# THE MAGIC PRINCIPLES OF THE ENNEAGRAM

*Discover Who You Really Are, Your True Needs and Those of Others by Understanding the 9 Personality Types and The Power of The Enneagram*

## Table of Contents

**Introduction ..................................................................... 5**
**Chapter One - Understanding the Enneagram ............... 8**
What the Enneagram Figure Means...................................... 8
How to Identify Your Personality Type................................ 12
About the Levels ................................................................. 13

**Chapter Two - The Reformer (Type 1).......................... 16**
Fifteen Signs You're a Reformer ......................................... 16
The Reformer: An Overview ............................................... 17
The Reformer Levels ........................................................... 18
The Reformer Wings........................................................... 23
Advice For The Reformer .................................................... 26

**Chapter Three – The Helper (Type 2) ........................... 28**
Fifteen Signs You're a Helper ............................................. 28
The Helper: An Overview.................................................... 29
The Helper Levels................................................................ 30
The Helper Wings ................................................................ 33
Advice for the Helper........................................................... 35

**Chapter Four – The Achiever (Type 3).......................... 37**
Fifteen Signs You're an Achiever......................................... 37
The Achiever: An Overview ................................................ 38
The Achiever Levels ............................................................ 39
The Achiever Wings ............................................................ 42
Advice for the Achiever ....................................................... 45

**Chapter Five - The Individualist (Type 4) ..................... 46**
Fifteen Signs You're An Individualist.................................. 46
The Individualist Overview ................................................. 48
The Individualist Levels ...................................................... 49
The Individualist Wings....................................................... 52
Advice for The individualist ................................................ 54

**Chapter Six - The Investigator (Type 5) ........................ 56**
Fifteen Signs You're An Investigator................................... 56

The Inspector Overview ............................................................. 57
The Investigator Levels .............................................................. 59
The Investigator Wings .............................................................. 61
Advice for The Investigator ....................................................... 63

**Chapter Seven - The Loyalist (Type 6) ............................................ 65**
Fifteen Signs You're A Loyalist ................................................. 65
The Loyalist Overview ............................................................... 67
The Loyalist Levels .................................................................... 68
The Loyalist Wings .................................................................... 71
Advice for The Loyalist .............................................................. 73

**Chapter Eight - The Enthusiast (Type 7) .......................................... 75**
Fifteen Signs You're an Enthusiast ............................................ 75
The Enthusiast Overview ........................................................... 76
The Enthusiast Levels ................................................................ 78
The Enthusiast Wings ................................................................ 80
Advice for The Enthusiast .......................................................... 85

**Chapter Nine - The Challenger (Type 8) ........................................... 87**
Fifteen Signs You're a Challenger ............................................. 87
The Challenger Overview .......................................................... 89
The Challenger Levels ............................................................... 90
The Challenger Wings ............................................................... 93
Advice for The Challenger ......................................................... 96

**Chapter Ten - The Peacemaker (Type 9) .......................................... 98**
Fifteen Signs You're a Peacemaker ........................................... 98
The Peacemaker Overview ........................................................ 99
The Peacemaker Levels ........................................................... 102
The Peacemaker Wings ........................................................... 105
Advice for The Peacemaker .................................................... 108

**Conclusion ............................................................................... 109**

# Introduction

The world in which we live is a complex place, teeming with so many different voices, influences and ideas. It can be somewhat of a challenge to remain centered and stay true to who you are, to actually know and understand who you truly are, and take appropriate action based on this vital self-knowledge.

Do you seek clarity in a world that can often feel confusing? Would you like to grow personally, with the confidence that you are growing in the right direction? Perhaps you seek a better understanding of your loved ones. A way to avoid conflict and to achieve more harmony. To learn which partners you are compatible with and to deepen those relationships. If so, the Enneagram might well provide the solution you have been seeking.

Modern theories relating to the Enneagram are variously credited to the teachings of George Gurdjieff, Oscar Ichazo and Claudio Naranjo. It is a system of nine different personality types and it combines the considerable benefits of both modern psychology and traditional wisdom. It can be used as a powerful tool for understanding ourselves and others. It has also been used extensively in the realms of both spirituality and business - specifically in the areas of team building, leadership development and communication skills.

In this book, you will learn the basic tenets and principles of the Enneagram and receive thorough and revealing outlines of each individual personality type. You will discover your own particular 'type' along the way - there are nine in all - and the various strengths and challenges that accompany this. You will come to understand how to use these strengths to your advantage and how to overcome and transcend the unique issues that your particular type might have to grapple with.

# Enneagram

For all of my life, I've held a deep passion for self-development and personality tests. It goes beyond everyday interest; my life has truly been shaped by my discoveries. And my deep understanding of the Enneagram has allowed me to read people in a way that most people cannot. By identifying my personality type, I finally became able to identify my true needs. If you don't know what your needs are, how can you ever hope to meet them?

I have discovered from personal experience that by digging deep and learning who I truly am, my life is richer and more meaningful. I am also capable of making much better decisions when it comes to the more important things in life. I am an Enneagram Type Four and this knowledge helps me to know my frailties, to nimbly walk around them and to capitalize on and give myself credit for my strengths. In a way, it makes it easier when I know there is a reason for it all. It is not my fault, it is because I am a Four!

This book can be used as a guide along your road to self-discovery. You can use it as a tool to understand yourself more deeply and to identify your dominant traits. It provides everything you need to know on how to deal with all your wonderful idiosyncrasies and to achieve personal growth along the way. The book can provide additional insight too. By identifying the 'types' of our significant others - be they friends, partners or family members - we achieve a better insight into how to make these relationships work and furthermore, how to deepen them. Communication can be improved and conflicts lessened.

People from all over the world and from every generation have given testimonials about the positive impact of the Enneagram on their lives. This can manifest in a whole range of ways. Examples include recognizing the mental patterns that underlie emotions. Developing self-awareness such as learning about the meaning of bodily sensations like tension. Understanding the strategies we use for self-preservation. Owning your own emotions and establishing boundaries. Allowing vulnerability and accessing your own innate wisdom.

# Enneagram

This book provides a definitive guide to all you need to know about the Enneagram and how to utilize the knowledge it provides. You will discover your type. Learn your potential strengths and weaknesses. Gain access to the power of self-understanding. You will have a deeper analysis and insight into who you really are and into the personalities of all of those around you. Imagine how useful it would be to gain insight into your prickly co-worker or your difficult boss! And in your romantic life: picture the advantage you will have in assessing potential partners and even avoiding repeating unhealthy relationship patterns from your past.

Life is short. Why waste time in confusion when clarity can be yours? The Enneagram and the insights it reveals can be an excellent place to start. It is said that an unexamined life is not worth living. The Enneagram can provide the awareness that is ultimately the key to all change and leads to far reaching benefits.

Unconscious behaviours and triggers are brought to the fore, enabling us to finally deal with them. Not only can you grow personally, but you can improve your relationships, both in the workplace and with friends and loved ones.

The information pertaining to the Enneagram that is contained in this book has led to life changing and far reaching positive consequences for many. Join the growing ranks of people who have experienced wonderful changes in their friendships, careers, romantic relationships and personal development.

Two thousand years ago, as pilgrims approached the sacred temple at Delphi, they were greeted by the sign: "Know Thyself." This sage advice is just as relevant today. Self-knowledge is power. But first you have to seek it. Then use it. This book can help you do just that.

# Chapter One - Understanding the Enneagram

There are many personality tests in the public domain. You may have heard of some of them. The Myers Briggs personality test is one of the most famous of these, and you might have taken this yourself. But I would venture to say that The Enneagram is more than a personality test. It would be more accurately described as an immensely powerful tool for personal, not to mention collective, transformation.

So just what is this enigma known as the Enneagram? To delve a little deeper into its true meaning and origins, we are first going to examine the symbol which represents it.

## What the Enneagram Figure Means

The Enneagram symbol or figure is made up of three individual shapes, each having its own separate meaning. We will first examine the underlying circle:

### The Circle

It will come as no surprise that the circle represents the wholeness or oneness of life - as in the Circle of Life. The circle also serves as a kind of container within which we conduct our lives. As we navigate our way through life, fragmentation can occur, often because of the ego. The goal is to reach awareness that we have never actually lost our wholeness.

### The Triangle

In many cultures, three is regarded as a mystical and magical number. This is sometimes known as the Law of Threes. This law holds that every phenomenon consists of three individual forces. When three forces are present, things start to happen. But with only one or two forces available, nothing at all happens. Each force has a different name. The first is known as the active or positive or motivating force. The second one is called the negative or passive or denying force and the third is named the neutralizing, facilitating or invisible force. As an esoteric law, the Law of Threes works both in our inner world and our outer world. You might be able to observe it in your interactions with other people.

There are numerous cultural examples of the Law of Threes. One of the most pervasive and one which the majority of people will be familiar with, is that of the concept of the holy trinity - the father, son and The Holy Spirit - which is espoused by the Christian tradition.

## The Hexad

The Hexad is a more unusual and irregular symbol which finds its origins in Sufism - the mystical branch of Islam. It is actually a six pointed figure but it follows seven points, from the start, through six changes of momentum, then back to its origin, which is considered the seventh point. It represents the Law of Seven, which is sometimes known as the law of octaves. It propounds that phenomena evolves in seven steps. Along with the Law of Threes, it was believed by Gurdjieff, a chief proponent of The Enneagram, that the Law of Seven was a global law and essential to his cosmology.

The Law of Seven states that the path of movement, either towards or away from anything, does not occur in a straight line. Rather, there are periods of striving, falling and striving again - a kind of rising and falling of energies along the way.

These three shapes are overlaid onto one another in order to create the Enneagram symbol. The lines on the Enneagram symbol show a path to a richer and fuller life. Self-observation is encouraged here, in order to avoid the different triggers of our personalities which might tend to lead one astray.

# Enneagram

The numbers - one to nine - on the Enneagram symbol, represent the nine different personality types. The relationship between the numbers are demonstrated by the lines that connect them together. Each number is only connected to two other numbers.

## About the Wings

No one person is made up purely of one personality type. Everyone is a mixture of their main type together with one of the two types next to it on the Enneagram figure. Whichever adjacent type that you most identify with is known as your 'wing.'

Your dominant wing is indicated by the higher score of one of the types that exists on either side of your basic type. For example, if your basic type is Three, your wing will be Two or Four, whichever one has the highest score. It is worth noting that the second highest overall score on your Enneagram test is not necessarily that of your wing.

The idea is that the wing types have an extra influence on your basic type.

## The Triads (or Centers)

The nine personality types of the Enneagram are arranged into three triads, otherwise known as centers. Three of the types are in the instinctive center (One, Eight and Nine), three in the feeling center (Two, Three and Four) and three in the thinking center, (Five, Six and Seven). The three personalities that occupy the same center share the same strengths and weaknesses as one another.

# Enneagram

Each triad or center is associated with a particular emotion. The instinctive center is associated with anger, whereas the feeling center tends to feel more shame. And the thinking center is linked to feelings of fear. Of course, each and every person can be subject to each and every emotion, but in each triad, the personalities associated with it are especially affected by that triad's emotional theme. You'll find that each personality type has a particular way of coping with its dominant emotion.

The three numbers within each triad or center have a pattern that they follow. The first number in each triad *expresses* the emotion that it is hyper-focused on. So types Eight, Two and Five express and externalize their emotions. This means that Eight externalizes anger, Two externalizes shame and Five externalizes fear.

This means that they either project the emotion outwardly or experience it outside themselves. When these personalities experience these emotions, they manifest right in front of us.

The second number in each center *represses* the emotion upon which it focuses. That is, Nine, Three and Six. So Nine represses anger, Three represses shame and Six represses fear. In other words, they do their best to pretend that the emotion doesn't exist for them.

The third number in each center *internalizes* the emotion it is most associated with. Thus, One, Four and Seven try to internalize their emotions. One internalizes anger, Four internalizes shame and Seven internalizes fear. These personalities experience these emotions inwardly or turn it in on themselves. This is different from repression because they still feel the emotion they are concealing, but they are choosing not to show it. This may lead these personality types, especially Four, to brood.

## How to Identify Your Personality Type

The upcoming chapters provide a comprehensive guide to the nine different personality types, set out in numerical order. Each chapter begins with a check list comprising of fifteen questions to ask yourself in order to ascertain whether or not you are likely to be that particular type.

It would be a good idea to keep a record of which personality type you tick off the most statements for. This practice should identify your personality type. In a similar way, keep track of which adjacent personality type you score the most for. This will be your dominant wing.

It is quite common to find a little of yourself in all of the nine Enneagram personality types, although one of them should stand out as being the closest to you. This is your basic type.

We are all familiar with the ongoing debate between nature and nurture. In terms of the Enneagram, experts agree that we are born with a dominant type. This inborn temperament seems to determine the ways in which we adapt to our early childhood environment.

People do not switch from one personality type to another. For instance, if you are born a One, you will stay a One for the entirety of your life. A few other points are worth bearing in mind. All the types apply equally to men and to women. And a larger number on the Enneagram scale is no better or worse than a lower number. In other words, an eight is no better than a three or vice versa. Each type has its own inherent strengths and weaknesses. No Enneagram personality type is better or worse than another. We should all strive to be our best selves rather than striving to emulate other types.

## About the Levels

Of course, not all the people from the same type will be exactly the same. This is obvious when we consider the diversity of the human beings we are surrounded with. So what is it that accounts for these differences?

Each personality type is made up of nine levels of development. This hypothesis was first reached by Don Riso in 1977. Riso, together with Russ Hudson, further developed the idea in the 1990s. The concept of the levels adds depth to our understanding of the Enneagram system and accounts both for the differences that arise between people of the same type and also how people can change, positively or negatively.

The levels of development provide deeper understanding to the explanation of the different elements contained within a personality type. This ties in with the complexity of human nature. The levels of development provide for us a kind of skeletal framework which allows us to see how all the traits of a particular type are interrelated, and how a healthy trait can become average, or can become unhealthy. Of course, this can work in the opposite direction also.

The levels show us that the personality is dynamic and ever changing. It helps us understand that people can change states within their personality, shifting within the spectrum of traits that make up their personality type.

It can help significantly in our understanding of others to assess whether someone is in their healthy, average or unhealthy level of functioning.

The nine levels of development are comprised of three levels in the healthy segment, three levels in the average segment and three levels in the unhealthy segment. Shades of grey abound.

# Enneagram

The continuum of the levels of development is as follows:

## **Healthy**

Level 1: The level of liberation

Level 2: The level of psychological capacity

Level 3: The level of social value

## **Average**

Level 4: The level of imbalance/social role

Level 5: The level of interpersonal control

Level 6: The level of overcompensation

## **Unhealthy**

Level 7: The level of violation

Level 8: The level of obsession and compulsion

Level 9: The level of pathological destructiveness

Try and be as honest as you can when it comes to assessing your own level. Even though this can sometimes expose uncomfortable truths, it is the surest path to personal growth.

Levels can be understood in terms of our capacity to be present. The further we move down the levels, the less present we are and the more we are identified with the ego and its negative patterns. The lower down the levels we go, the more defensive, compulsive and destructive we become. We tend to be less free, less self-aware, and act on a more sub-conscious level.

Conversely, as we move up the levels, we become more and more present. We are less destructive and increasingly free and open. We are far more self-aware and astute. We are less likely to get caught up in negativity.

Becoming more present allows us to be more objective about our personality and we become adept at self-observation. This makes us more effective in all areas of our lives, whether that be relationships or our career. It can bring genuine peace and joy to whatever it is that we are doing.

## Chapter Two - The Reformer (Type 1)

*Also known as the Perfectionist*

**Fifteen Signs You're a Reformer**

1. You strive to make the world a better place in which to live. You are capable of seeing, in clear detail, what is wrong with a situation and you are prepared to take the necessary steps to rectify matters.

2. You possess a very strong sense that you have a life purpose or a mission to fulfill.

3. Other people often describe you as being responsible, dependable and brimming over with common sense. They can also sometimes accuse you of having no feelings. (You *do* have feelings – you're just keeping them all in!)

4. You think you have to do everything perfectly, going so far as to think that *you* yourself have to be perfect.

5. You are highly self-disciplined - sometimes to a fault. You have little to no trouble sticking to a schedule or routine.

6. You hate feeling stagnant and you always ache to be useful in some way.

7. You feel you have to keep a lid on all your very strong wants and needs.

8. It is vitally important to you that you 'do the right thing.'

9. You have an intense fear of making mistakes or blunders.

10. You tend to experience tension in your shoulders, neck and jaw.

11. It sometimes takes you longer than the average person to complete a task, which is, of course, because of your exceptional eye for detail.

12. You can be very critical of yourself and others.

13. You may experience disappointment and frustration at those times when reality does not meet your expectations.

14. You hold yourself to very high standards of excellence.

Does this sound anything like you?

## The Reformer: An Overview

Perfectionism can be a double-edged sword. On the one hand, it can cause impressive and wonderfully satisfying results. On the other, it can lead to wounding self-criticism and even inaction, where the perfectionist might not even begin a task for fear of failure.

Type One in The Enneagram model is not lacking in the least when it comes to admirable traits such as reliability, honesty, common sense, integrity and nobility. In fact, this type can be downright heroic. They could, however, learn to be kinder to themselves. Although lowering your standards is not usually to be recommended, Ones could sometimes benefit from taking such advice, as the expectations they heap upon themselves - and others - can be unrealistically and punishingly high.

This type wishes to make the world a better place, and what's not to like about that?! High ideals are the order of the day, coupled with a strong sense of purpose. These people get things done and done right!

You might also recognize a One by their fastidious attention to detail: that go-to co-worker who you can always rely on. Granted, they may take longer than most to complete the task, but the end result will be undoubtedly flawless. Or it might be the friend with the incredible self-discipline, who will keep to the diet or the exercise regime and whose gym membership will be used beyond the third week in January.

If you want to keep in a One's good books, make sure you keep your promises. *Never* say you are going to do something and then back out or forget about it. This is a complete no-no and breaks their ethical code. These good people would never do the same to you! And don't forget to take things seriously. This type does not appreciate a flippant attitude. It will surprise and delight them if you join them in speculating about how things can be improved in the world, and you will make all their dreams come true by actually taking action. Encourage them also to be less critical of themselves. Teach them that a little self-kindness goes a long way. Above all, a One needs a friend who can coax them to have fun and to take life - and themselves - a little less seriously.

## The Reformer Levels

**Healthy**

**Heroism**

# Enneagram

Type Ones on The Enneagram are the stuff that heroes are made of. A man by the name of Gandhi comes to mind. He embodied the qualities of the One at his or her best, in his capacity for extraordinary wisdom and discernment. His humanity inspired immense loyalty and made him a great leader that thousands of people felt compelled to follow. And we need look no further than Joan of Arc for a historical example of a One who uplifted many and created change through the courage of her conviction and willingness to self sacrifice.

Not every One can be a Gandhi or a Joan of Arc, but within their own private sphere of influence, no matter how big or small, they can often perform acts of everyday heroism.

## Practical Action

It is one thing to have lofty ideals. It is quite another to act in accordance with them. But the One is a master of practical action, striving always to be useful, to fix the things that they consider broken and to fulfil their powerful mission in life. These people put their money where their mouth is. They have no qualms around making personal sacrifices to serve a higher cause.

## Loyalty

The Reformer will not say one thing and then do another. They are impeccable with their word. Neither will they make promises to do something and then not do it. If you are lucky enough to have the friendship of a One, you know that you have someone who will always have your back.

## Attention to Detail

# Enneagram

A One will not leave a job half-done. Neither will they turn in a shoddy project. They always strive for excellence, in thought, word and deed. This type is always pushing the envelope and raising standards - for themselves and the world in which they live. Consider these prominent Ones in the areas of politics, business and entertainment. Such people as: Nelson Mandela, Michelle Obama, Anita Roddick (The Body Shop), Martha Stewart, Dame Maggie Smith and Meryl Streep, Confucious, Margaret Thatcher, Plato, George Bernard Shaw, Noam Chomsky, Emma Thompson, Jane Fonda, Jerry Seinfeld, George Harrison, Hilary Clinton, Jimmy Carter, Prince Charles.

**Integrity**

A One's deep sense of integrity makes him or her an excellent teacher and, in general, a witness and proponent of the truth. They are principled to the core and will uphold these principles even at the cost of their own safety or comfort. You can trust them to always do the right thing, even if this goes against conventional wisdom or public opinion. The Reformer will not be swayed from what he or she believes to be right and good.

**Neutral or Average**

**Dissatisfaction**

The Reformer at this level thinks it is up to them to fix everything. They feel they know how everything 'should' be done and that it is their absolute duty to tell everybody else what they should do too!

**Rigidity**

This rigidity is caused by the fear of making a mistake. Everything has to be exactly right. There is no margin for error whatsoever, either for the Reformer themselves or for those around them.

**Overly critical**

The Reformer directs this criticism - not just at him or herself - but at others too. They feel the need to correct people constantly, and not in an especially sensitive way! Very low level of satisfaction.

**Unhealthy**

**Hell is other people!**

It's not always easy being a Reformer. You will constantly encounter those with different value systems to your own and this might well upset your high-minded ideals and insistence on excellence. It may lead you to be self-righteous, intolerant, dogmatic or inflexible. You might severely judge others for their inability to see things in the same way that you do.

**Obsession**

There is a risk that Ones can become obsessive in nature. This can manifest itself in a number of ways. One of these is in the area of diet and nutrition. In extreme cases, the Reformer's quest for self-control might lead to conditions such as anorexia and bulimia. Some might also resort to alcohol in order to alleviate the stress that they put themselves under. Obsessive Compulsive Disorder is also a danger to this type.

**Anger**

The Reformer can get angry very easily and this anger can often have a tinge of self-righteousness to it. Offense may be taken easily, from other people's refusal to do what the One believes to be right. This anger - however righteous - can unfortunately have the effect of alienating others. This is a great pity, as Ones often have a very valid point to make. Repressing this anger is not the answer either, as this might manifest in health issues such as high blood pressure or ulcers.

**Depression**

This is a fate that can befall a person with a dominant Type One personality, when the trait takes an unhealthy turn. A less than healthy Reformer can be extremely condemnatory, not to mention cruel, to themselves and others. Depressions, breakdowns and suicide attempts are the worst possible outcome here.

**Unrealistically High Standards**

Enneagram Type Ones can struggle with intense disappointment when reality does not match up to their expectations. It can make them appear overly negative or critical of other family members, friends or co-workers. It can make them very harsh task masters - pedantic and unforgiving. It is not pleasant to be on the receiving end of an unhealthy One's constant criticism and disappointment at your efforts.

**But it's not all doom and gloom!**

So, if you are a One - a Perfectionist, a Reformer - how can you best avoid the potential pitfalls and instead bring out the best in what your personality type has to offer?

## The Reformer Wings

**Type One with a Two wing (1W2)**

What do you get when you cross a Type One with a Type Two? Well, for a start, the One becomes less repressed and a little more emotionally balanced by the two's directedness and desire to please others.

This is often a very neat and tidy-looking person. The One gives them a propensity for perfectionism and the Two makes them more sensitive to criticism. In other words, they don't want to be criticized about their appearance. So their hair will be perfect and clothing will be just so. They might hold themselves very correctly and come across as having rather a condescending attitude.

This subtype is very hard on his or herself. They will make every effort to do the right thing and if they can also manage to please others in the process, that's even more preferable.

The healthy version of a One with a Two wing is a more relaxed version of a full One with less of an inclination to be righteously judgmental. They can actually believe and admit that they might not always be right!

The One enjoys correcting others. With the influence of the Two, the corrections become more helpful and less intrusive. They are also better able to tolerate differences with the benefit of the Two wing.

If the Reformer with the Two wing happens to experience a kind of spiritual awakening, he or she can become a most inspiring teacher who can bring joy and compassion to their practice. One is wise and Two is loving. At their best, this sub type can be a sterling friend who always seems to know the right thing to say or do.

But oh dear! Things can take a turn for the worse when the Reformer's not so emotionally healthy and mature. The One's perfectionism combined with the Two's pride can lead to trouble. It can amount to great inner conflict. Self-critical introspection goes into overdrive and may be accompanied by fits of rage which descend into self-judgement and remorse.

When severely unhealthy, the anger and pride combine to create despair. Here, the One with a Two wing will punish themselves endlessly and suicide might even be the end result.

It is not surprising the Reformer with a Two wing might enjoy work that involves helping other people become perfect. Examples of such would be teachers, dieticians and judges.

**Type One with a Nine wing (1W9)**

The combination of the perfectionism and judgement of Type One with the withdrawal from stress of Type Nine makes for a quiet, conservative and somewhat repressed sub type. They do not show a lot of emotion and they will come across as quite strict, quiet and practical. They are slow to express their views also but will usually act from principled judgement.

They can, of course, shine when emotionally healthy and mature. Here, they will learn to access an inner warmth and be capable of bringing it to the fore. Although they might still be a little judgmental, they allow for the fact that they are capable of getting it wrong at times. And anyway, it doesn't really matter that much after all. They learn at this stage to control the propensity of the Nine to withdraw under stress and this allows them to participate in life more fully. They are gentle, responsible, fun-loving and capable of relaxing and just letting go.

At their very best, they will be ever more joyful and participate in life with much gusto. They will have high self-esteem at this level. The wisdom of the One will merge with the selflessness of the Nine and can allow them to obtain significant spiritual advancement.

But this sub type can be unhealthy too and when they are, they might try to exert too much control over their emotions which will lend to them a physical rigidity punctuated by fissions of explosive energy.

Repressed emotions are ever present under the surface and they will come across as "nervy" types. They will be hostile and withdrawn and suffer from self-hatred. They might be highly suspicious and engage in passive-aggressive behaviour. Most of this will be bottled up.

If things disintegrate even further, they can come across as robotic and ritualistic. Anxiety about performing routines just right can become extreme. They may descend into psychosis and become paralyzed with inaction.

This variant of the One stands upright and offers few, but genuine, smiles. It is possible that they are drawn to work that expresses their talent for performing precise tasks, such as accountancy or computer programming.

# Enneagram

## Advice For The Reformer

I know you didn't ask for advice, but we're going to give it to you anyway! As a Reformer, you probably don't feel you need any counsel, because of your higher than average sense of right and wrong and your intense feeling of purpose. And you are right, to a point. We each need to follow our own star. However, we all have our weaknesses too, and it can be very useful at times to have a second eye, as it were, to give us a greater sense of perspective.

1. Keep in mind that not everyone will see the world in such black and white terms as you do. There are numerous shades of grey and sometimes you need to make allowances for middle-ground.

2. Find a healthy way to express and release your anger, one that doesn't involve another human having to feel the full extent of your wrath but at the same time, means you don't repress it all, which could lead to serious health problems for you. It may also help to find less reasons to be angry. Accepting other people's imperfections, perhaps! Don't forget that people can be chaotic. If someone turns up late for an appointment, it doesn't necessarily mean that they disrespect you or don't value your time. They might just be struggling with the messiness of their own lives. Be less critical of others. And while you're at it, be less critical of yourself too!

3. Keep in mind the famous serenity prayer: Grant me the serenity to accept the things I cannot change, the courage to change the things I can and the wisdom to know the difference.

4. Be cognizant that you have a tendency to store tension in your body, particularly in your jawline, neck and shoulders. Consider taking steps to counteract this, such as meditation, massage or other relaxation techniques. And why not try to have fun! This is a proven and excellent path to relaxation. After all, nobody likes a martyr!

5. It is possible that you had parents with very high expectations of you. If this is the case, perhaps it is now time to re-parent yourself and show yourself more softness and kindness. Remember: 'Angels fly because they take themselves lightly.' You don't have to take yourself so seriously all the time. And remind yourself often that everyone makes mistakes, including you. You are not a failure if you make a mistake. This is how we learn. Acceptance of this is key. Furthermore, it is perfectly acceptable to have human emotions and impulses. And sometimes 'good enough' is good enough. Perfection is an illusion. So forgive yourself for your imperfections. Forgiveness is a gift to yourself even more so than to the one that you are forgiving.

6. You often feel that the weight of the world is on your shoulders. Thankfully, it is not. You are just one person and you are doing just fine.

7. Trust your inner guidance and most of all, trust life.. Your tendency to see so clearly where things need to be improved, can make you blind to the many things that are right with the world. If you look more closely, you will recognize that things are often working out.

8. Try not to be too disappointed or impatient if those around you don't change immediately in accordance with what you might have taught them. It does not mean that you are not a gifted teacher, but rather that everyone develops at their own pace. Patience is a virtue!

Above all, don't stop being who you are. There is a reason you were born this way so find out why and make the most of it!

## Chapter Three – The Helper (Type 2)

*Also known as the Giver*

### Fifteen Signs You're a Helper

1. You love to be involved in other people's lives.

2. You always feel the urge to put other people before yourself.

3. You tend to give a lot of time and money to charity.

4. You are able to see the good in your fellow humans.

5. You need to be needed.

6. You can totally exhaust yourself, running around doing things for other people.

7. You may feel offended if someone refuses your offer of help.

8. You require appreciation for the things you do for others.

9. Your friends describe you as being someone who is always willing to go that extra mile.

10. You sometimes forget to look after yourself and this can lead to physical or emotional burnout.

11. You don't consider life worth living unless you are giving to others in some way.

12. You have a deep seated fear of worthlessness.

13. You might well be a wonderful cook and homemaker!

14. You might have a tendency to use food to 'stuff' down your feelings.

15. Personal relationships are of the utmost importance to you.

Do any of the above points ring a bell?

## The Helper: An Overview

The focus of Type Two of the Enneagram is very much on relationships. It is what makes these people tick - making connections and then empathizing with the feelings and needs of others. However, they can go too far in this tendency and can twist themselves into all sorts of shapes just to win approval from their peers. Co-dependency is a trap that type two can sometimes fall prey to, priding themselves on what they can do for other people and feeling shame at those times when they can't actually help or support others.

In a way, our culture nurtures and awards the typical behavior of a Type Two, in that it encourages us to believe that our self-worth comes from what we do for other people. Women especially are taught this kind of behaviour. Although being kind to others is, of course, laudable, the Helper must guard against a tendency to smother or overwhelm. And it is never good for someone to deny their own personal interests and needs. Burnout or martyrdom may ensue! So if you are a Two, you would do well to balance your impulse to assist others with your own self-care.

As a Helper, love is your highest goal. You pride yourself on selflessness. You are often extroverted and may also have the knack for creating a comfortable and welcoming home for your family. You are huge on empathy and often a genuinely caring person with a very warm heart. You are friendly and generous. Just make sure that your motives for helping others are pure.

Examples of famous twos include such luminaries as Bishop Desmond Tutu, Byron Katie, John Denver, Dolly Parton, Eleanor Roosevelt, Luciano Pavarotti, Stevie Wonder, Elizabeth Taylor, Martin Sheen, Bobby McFerrin, Lionel Richie, Nancy Reagan, Josh Groban, Paula Abdul and Barry Manilow.

Type two has been given the name 'The Helper' for a reason: these people are either the most genuinely helpful to others *or* the most in need to see themselves as helpful.

## The Helper Levels

As with every other type, Helpers differ in maturity and psychological health. We will explore the state of The Helper at healthy, neutral and unhealthy stages.

# Enneagram

## Healthy

### Unconditionally Loving

The Helper at his or her best is capable of giving truly unconditional love. He or she is humble and unselfish, feeling it is a privilege to give and to be meaningfully involved in the lives of others.

### Empathetic

Empathy is the helper's middle name. This type can be spilling over with compassion and concern for their fellow human beings. In addition, they have learnt the art and value of forgiveness.

### Encouraging

The Helper at this level can easily appreciate the goodness of other people. They have learnt to balance service with self-care and give for all the right reasons.

## Neutral

### The People-Pleaser

An air of desperation can sometimes creep into Type Two's desire to help others. A kind of clinging rather than closeness. They might be tempted to give compliments that are not entirely genuine but instead meant to gain favor from the person they are flattering.

### The Co-Dependent

This stage involves possessiveness and intrusiveness. The need to be needed can become so strong that the Type Two can be deeply controlling yet tell themselves that they are actually being loving. They want others to be dependent on them and often wear themselves out with needlessly self-sacrificial behaviour.

**Self-Importance**

A heightened sense of self-importance is probable at this level. Martyrdom can really kick in with the Helper believing that they are being far more helpful than they actually are! Type Two at this level might feel that he or she is indispensable when they are really not, and this can cause them to be patronizing and overbearing.

**Unhealthy**

**Manipulation**

Oh dear! Things start to get nasty when Type Twos exhibit unhealthy behavior patterns. At this level, a Two may well pile on the guilt, highlighting how much they believe people owe them for all they've done. This level displays the general attitude of "How *could* you after everything I've done for you?!" If people do not show the requisite level of appreciation, they might undermine them in an aggressive way. At this level, the Two will lack the self-awareness to see how unreasonable and damaging their behavior is. They may also begin to use food and drugs as a way of self-medication.

**Domineering**

At this unsavory level, the Two feels that everybody they've "helped" - whether or not that person asked for that help in the first place or actually wanted it at all! - owes them an enormous debt of gratitude and therefore must "pay" in whatever way the Two deems appropriate. There is a negative sense of entitlement where this type asserts the hold they feel they have earned.

**Chronic Resentment**

Such resentment arises when an unhealthy Two steps fully into victim mode and feels unjustly abused by those they have "helped." Because of this, they feel justified in displaying all sorts of irrational and aggressive behavior. All these highly negative emotions can result in serious health problems, both physical and mental. Not a happy place to be! Both for the Helper and for those around them.

# The Helper Wings

As previously discussed, a type's wings are derived from the two number types that are physically beside it on the circumference of the Enneagram figure. For the Helper, the Reformer (Type 1) and the Achiever (Type 3) are possible wings or influencers on the personality.

**Type Two with a One Wing (2W1)**

We have already seen that Type Ones are perfectionists at heart. On the plus side, they are responsible, conscientious, progress-oriented and potentially heroic. Their shadow side can be hyper-critical, this being directed both at themselves and others. At times, they can also be resentful and judgemental. So what can a Type Two with a One wing look like?

All going well, this combination of types leads to a person who is loving, warm and generous, as you would expect, but the One influence adds resolve and moral obligation. The desire to do good is thus heightened by the number One's motivation to do everything 'right.'

The focus of the One's generosity becomes a drive for social justice under the influence of the Reformer. The desire to improve the world is genuine. The Helper with this wing is also more willing to take on the unglamorous tasks that other people usually eschew, for the sake of the common good. The influence of the One on the Two can imbue them with a stronger backbone and a better awareness of where feelings might threaten to overtake their good judgment.

But, as always, there is a flip side. Destructive perfectionism could rear its ugly head, causing the helper to think that they, and they alone, know best. This makes them imposing, preachy and intrusive. They may also judge themselves very severely. A potential negative side of this combination of types can also be that the Two has even more trouble recognizing her own needs and feelings and strongly believes that her own personal desire is selfish and should be quashed.

**Type Two with a Three Wing (1W3)**

We will examine Type Three in detail later on. For the time being, here is a brief summary:

Type Three is variously known as the Achiever or the Performer. As the name suggests, these people tend to be ambitious, enthusiastic and adaptable. They are driven and like nothing more than to accomplish goals and receive validation from others.

A Three wing makes the Two more social and good-humored than a One wing tends to do. It is all about the heart and feelings when it comes to this pairing. Relationships are sought and valued. This combination of types often possesses much charisma and others enjoy their company greatly. They are natural and gracious hosts or hostesses and love to throw parties and gather friends together for celebrations. They have great generosity of spirit and love to give of themselves for the betterment of others.

In times of stress, however, the 2W3, who perceives other's feelings so strongly, can be overwhelmed by the needs of others and even their own repressed emotions. Because types Two and Three both belong in the heart-centered triad, they lack the self-awareness that the influence of a head or body (such as One) type would lend to them. This particular marriage of types can lead to over-sensitivity if they are on the receiving end of criticism. Their sense of pride can become over-inflated, which might lead to authoritarian behaviour and outbursts of anger.

## Advice for the Helper

1. Take care to look after your own self-care. You are so busy empathizing with other people and supporting them in their needs, that you forget your own needs in the process. Your own requirements are just as important as everybody else's. It is important to set and maintain your own personal boundaries and to ensure that you get adequate rest, exercise and proper nutrition. Do not change yourself in order to win approval from another. By being yourself and establishing boundaries, you can give to others more authentically, and you can only be of real service to others if you are balanced, healthy and centered within yourself.

# Enneagram

2. Before you help somebody, consider whether or not they actually need or want your help in the first place. Have they asked for your assistance? Make sure that you are not just imposing your ideas of the way things should be upon them and interfering unnecessarily. Furthermore, it is not up to you to demand gratitude or decide the manner in which such gratitude is expressed. Instead, try asking people directly what it is they really need. Just because you can sense the need of another, does not necessarily mean that they would like you to step in and 'solve' all their problems for them. You must be willing to accept a "no, thank you" if that is what's forthcoming. This should not be taken as rejection.

3. In the event of you doing something nice for someone, there is no need whatsoever to remind them of it. This is a temptation you need to resist. It will only make the other party question your motivation for helping them in the first place and will cause them to be uncomfortable. They might also withdraw from you altogether, if you choose to behave in this way. Let kindness be its own reward!

4. Understand that people express their affection and appreciation in lots of different ways. Just because it is in a manner that is not instantly recognizable to you and not necessarily a way which you would have chosen yourself, does not mean that they do not care. Learn to recognize the different manifestations of love.

5. Make sure you are honest about your own motives and that you are not lying to yourself about why you are helping someone. If you are just doing it in order to receive gratitude, this is not a healthy motive and you might well be setting yourself up for disappointment. You must guard against co-dependency at all times.

# Chapter Four – The Achiever (Type 3)

*Also known as the Performer*

## Fifteen Signs You're an Achiever

1. You like to get things done and are more than willing to work hard to achieve your goals.

2. You can find it hard to slow down and you might struggle to find time to relax.

3. Patience is not one of your virtues!

4. Those around you describe you as a "Type A" personality.

5. You tend to store tension in your chest and heart area.

6. You have no problem setting aside your hobbies to chase success in your primary goal.

7. You love a challenge and relish throwing everything you have into meeting that challenge.

8. If at first you don't succeed, you will try, try, try again.

9. Your biggest fear is failure and this can cause you much stress and anxiety.

10. You focus on appearance. You can become overly concerned with your image and how other people perceive you.

11. A question you are often asked is, "How do you achieve so much?"

12. You very much enjoy a sense of completion and accomplishment. There's nothing like ticking boxes off your to-do list!

13. You are highly competitive and this is something that drives you.

14. You are 'self-made' in some way, having got to where you are in life by hard work and determined pursuit of your goals.

15. You have a lot of energy and others might describe you as having a zest for life which they often find attractive.

What do you think? Have many of the above points resonated with you?

## The Achiever: An Overview

As the name suggests, the Type Three on the Enneagram is all about success. It is of vital importance to this type that their success is acknowledged. The Achiever requires this validation in order to feel worthy. They are highly focused, hard-working and competitive. These goals are often in the business world but they are not restricted to this sphere by any means. The Three is commonly a 'self-made' success, often skilled in the art of networking. Generally extroverted, the Achiever can sometimes be charismatic. There is a boundless energy and plenty of drive. Their shadow side is their secret fear of failure.

The Achiever, or the Performer, is frequently image-conscious and as such, can be slow to let his or her real self be shown. This can make intimacy difficult. The Three fears others getting too close lest they discover what they are *really* like.

Because of the Type Three's strong requirement for external validation, they sometimes make the error of chasing external success while ignoring their deeper needs and desires. The Achiever needs to guard against falling in to such a trap.

Notable Three's from the worlds of history, politics, sports and the arts include Bill Clinton, Arnold Schwarzenegger, Oprah Winfrey, Madonna, Lady Gaga, Will Smith, Augustus Caesar, Tony Blair, Andy Warhol, Elvis Presley, Barbra Streisand, Richard Gere, Reese Witherspoon, Anne Hathaway, Justin Bieber, Jon Bon Jovi, Paul McCartney, Lance Armstrong, O.J,Simpson, Truman Capote, Muhammad Ali, Emperor Constantine, Prince William, Carl Lewis, Tony Robbins, Deepack Chopra, Michael Jordan, Sting, Brooke Shields, Tiger Woods, Taylor Swift, Tom Cruise, Demi Moore, Courtney Cox and Kevin Spacey.

## The Achiever Levels

**Healthy**

**Authenticity**

So genuine and appealing, the Three at their best is literally dripping with gentleness and benevolence. They have learned to fully accept themselves and to listen to their own internal guidance systems. These Threes are everything they appear to be as they have come to understand that they have nothing to hide. They are modest when it comes to their innate strengths and achievements and they are typically big-hearted people with a delightfully self-deprecating humour.

**Competence**

The high self-esteem of a healthy Three assists them in believing in themselves and their own capabilities. This type is self-assured with plenty of energy to get the job done and get it right. There is an intrinsic self-belief and a deep awareness of their own value as human beings. They are competent and confident enough to adapt to all sorts of situations and remain gracious and charming in the process. Many people will be naturally drawn to a healthy Three.

**Ambitious**

These Threes are ambitious in the very best sense of the word. Never ruthless, just eager to be the best version of themselves and to fulfill their potential. Self-improvement is a driving force for these people. The healthy Achiever has it in him or her to become an outstanding human, possessing a tremendous amount of admirable qualities. Other people tend to admire them greatly and try to emulate them. This makes the healthy Three a master motivator.

**Neutral**

**Driven**

The average Type Three sets great store in doing their job well. Unfortunately, at this level, their motivation for this can be slightly less healthy and based more frequently on an abject terror of failure. They worry very much about what other people think of them and base their self-worth on the achievement of goals. It is said that comparison is the thief of joy. It certainly is for this type. This less than healthy Three will compare his or herself with others in a quest for their own status and self-worth. This is the level of the social climber or the one who believes that a career is everything.

**Image-Consciousness**

The Achiever can care far too much about how he or she is perceived by others. This can cause them to be "phony" in some ways as they try to conform with the real or imagined expectations of others. They can certainly excel in practicality and efficiency but they risk losing touch with their feelings in their desire to impress. This can lead to issues with intimacy.

**Self-Promotion**

The intense desire to impress others can cause the Three, at this level of maturity, to promote themselves ceaselessly and aggressively. They might elevate their achievements to this cause. It might feel a little like the childish tendency to say "look at me!" Inflated notions of themselves may arise and they may come across as arrogant and full of contempt, but this is just an attempt to disguise their jealousy.

**Unhealthy**

**Fear of Failure**

The Achiever at this level is willing to do or say whatever they consider necessary to preserve their image. Fear of failure and humiliation is intense at this point and can lead them to exploitative and opportunistic behaviours. They will be extremely jealous of another person's success and will strive to preserve their fragile illusion of superiority at all costs.

**Deception**

These folks can become so terrified at the thought of their mistakes and misdeeds being exposed that they will resort to all sorts of devious behaviours to cover up such failings. This means, of course, that the Achiever at this unhealthy level can absolutely not be trusted. They might betray or sabotage somebody just to get one up on them and their jealous states can border on delusional.

**Narcissism**

This is the Three at their absolute worst, when their actions correspond with the description of the Narcissistic Personality Disorder. They will stop at nothing to ruin another person's happiness and their destructiveness can become obsessive. The vindictiveness of the profoundly unhealthy Three can border on the psychopathic.

## The Achiever Wings

**Type Three with a Two Wing (3W2)**

When you envisage the "typical" salesperson, you might well be picturing the Type Three with a Two wing. The Achiever's desire to be admired overtakes the Type Two's desire to please others and make them feel good. Although, if it's possible, they may well do both. This variety of the number Three is usually extroverted and can come across as attractive and even seductive. Their persona is cheerful and calm and they will be keen to show their best side and want to be perceived as having it together emotionally.

The influence of the Two wing on the Three personality, can make their "shine" more genuine. At best, this variety of the Three is big on self-observation and likely to be a humble type. They'll also be friendly and likeable with great social skills that cause others to enjoy being around them. The Two wing tempers the Three's hunger to always be the winner. Genuine feelings come to the fore and powerful bonds of friendship can and will be formed.

A healthy Type Three with a Two wing can become an excellent motivational speaker, capable of inspiring great confidence and optimism in others. Uplifting and positive - think Tony Robbins or Oprah Winfrey at their best.

However, when unhealthy, a brittle vanity can come into play for the Achiever with a Two wing. They can lose touch with their genuine innermost feelings while instead constructing a false emotional facade. Self-promotion can become pushy and aggressive, resulting in a lose-lose situation for all involved. They might appear nice and quiet on the outside but the internal reality could be quite unpleasant and destructive.

As outer appearance is important, the 3W2 will typically dress well and in accordance with the latest mainstream fashion. This is because they will want to appeal to the largest possible audience. They might be drawn to "glamorous" work - perhaps on stage, TV, radio, or a high profile position in the business world.

**Type Three with a Four Wing (3W4)**

Although the Achiever with a Four wing would still like to be admired, they would prefer that this be for their uniqueness rather than appealing to the general masses - a select following rather than mass appeal is what they are aiming for.

The Four wing will tend to make the Three more introverted and less comfortable in social situations, although because of the still dominant Type Three personality, they will be able to hide this with their social competence. They will still be able to hold it all together in times of pressure.

A healthy and mature Achiever with a Four wing is compassionate, gentle and competent. This variant is wise and socially responsible and highly effective in accomplishing their goals, all the while remaining intuitive. A suitable job for this type would be as a career counsellor or a business mentor.

At their absolute best, the Type Three with a Four wing is quietly self-assured while possessed of stunning emotional insight. They teach through example, influencing others through compassionate action. They can be found at the top of organizations or behind the scenes, inspiring others to perform their best.

It is an entirely different story when the Achiever with a Four wing is immature and unhealthy. A lack of balance here will make the Three-influenced drive for success compulsive, while at the same time causing the introspection of the Four to get out of hand. Manipulation comes to the fore and the desire to help is no longer coming from a good place. They are not so great socially and may also indulge in self-deception. They might feel a compulsive need to tell other people about their accomplishments. At their worst, they can be destructive to the self and others.

They like to appear both attractive and unique, wanting to be trend-setters rather than slavishly following the latest fashion. The 3W4 variant is typically drawn to quite showy professions, such as music, politics, broadcasting, the stage, the fashion industry and the sales side of business.

## Advice for the Achiever

1. Take a break every now and then from the relentless pursuit of your goals! Your health will benefit and so will your levels of happiness. And let's not forget your loved ones, who will all be pleased to have more time with you. Your goals will still be waiting for you when you wake up from a good night's sleep or return from a holiday. And you will feel refreshed and more effective than ever. Not to mention, nicer to be around. Ambition and determination can be sterling qualities, but they must be tempered by periods of rest which, additionally, allow time for you to reconnect deeply with your inner needs and feelings.

2. Try to be completely honest with yourself. Threes can sometimes get so caught up in trying to play to the peanut gallery that they lose touch with what they really need to be happy. Take time to consider what success actually means to you. What are your values? What makes you happy? Only when you truly connect with the reality of who you are, can you achieve real freedom.

3. As intimacy can sometimes be a challenge for you, it is worth taking the time and trouble to connect with a few chosen people on a deeper level. This takes self-awareness and the willingness to relax and practice appreciation for those you love.

4. It will benefit you greatly to become involved in projects that are unrelated to your ultimate ambition or career goals. It will take you outside of yourself in a healthy way and transcend your preoccupation with the opinions of others.

# Chapter Five - The Individualist (Type 4)

*Also known as The Romantic*

## Fifteen Signs You're An Individualist

1. You need a lot of time alone to recharge.

2. You may be an artist – not just a visual artist but perhaps also a dancer, a writer or a musician.

3. You have a tendency to feel melancholy and may get depressed when times get rough.

4. You sometimes feel haunted by the thought that something is missing from your life and this contributes to a deep sense of longing.

5. Authenticity is all important to you, both in your work and in your relationships.

6. You view yourself as being fundamentally different to other people.

# Enneagram

7. You are likely to be brutally honest and do not tend to hide your true feelings or motivations from yourself or from others.

8. You are willing to reveal things about yourself that most would never reveal for fear of being embarrassed or ashamed.

9. You have a deep yearning to connect with other people and you tend to feel misunderstood.

10. You've had more than one person in your life tell you that you're 'complicated' or 'weird.'

11. You suffer from low self-esteem and sometimes feel very alone in the world.

12. You are a highly sensitive person, and you have a hard time letting go of past hurts.

13. You'd rather have one close friendship than a hundred superficial ones.

14. Others sometimes accuse you of being moody.

15. Artist or not, you love to surround yourself with art and beautiful things.

Are lots of alarm bells going off in your head right now?

## The Individualist Overview

Type Four on the Enneagram likes to think of him or herself as different or unique, indeed basing their very identity on such uniqueness. Feeling different is a double-edged sword to this type. On the one hand, it can cause them to feel special and superior and on the other, isolated and alone.

The Individualist will often be drawn to the arts. They might make a career in this area, becoming dancers, writers, visual artists, musicians or sculptors, for instance. Or maybe they will work closely with artists, perhaps managing museums or galleries or bringing arts to education. Or perhaps they will express this aspect of themselves in the way that they dress or present themselves, or simply in the idiosyncratic lifestyles that they lead.

The sensitivity of this type is heightened and they are emotionally complex souls. Authenticity is all important to the Achiever and he or she longs to be appreciated for his or her own authentic self. This type has no capacity for or interest in shallow relationships. They often feel unappreciated or misunderstood by others and, in these circumstances, will tend to withdraw from the world.

The inner life of the Four is rich and they will spend a lot of time immersed in their own internal world. This activity is important to them and will help them to process their inner feelings. Sometimes, they can express their inner lives in artistic ways. But it is important that they guard against withdrawing from real life completely.

Fours can be haunted by the notion that something fundamental is missing from their lives and this leaves them with a sense of longing, which can morph into melancholy. In times of great stress, this can develop into full blown depression. Self-absorption to an unhealthy level is a trap they can fall into.

It is important for the Individualist/Romantic to strive to be their own savior instead of looking to others to rescue them. They must learn to stand on their own two feet. Be your own rescue, number Four!

Examples of luminaries throughout history who have been Type Fours include: Rumi, Tchaikovsky, Anne Frank, Frida Kahlo, Rudolf Nureyov, Joni Mitchell, Leonard Cohen, Jackie Kennedy Onassis, Chopin, Gustav Mahler, Edgar Allen Poe, Virginia Wolfe, Anais Nin, Anne Rice, Martha Graham, Hank Williams, J.D. Salinger, Tennessee Williams, Billie Holiday, Cher, Alanis Morrisetter, Florence Welch, from Florence and The Machine, Stevie Nicks, Judy Garland, Cat Stevens, Annie Lennox, Amy WInehouse, Johnny Depp, Nicholas Cage, Angelina Jolie, Marlon Brando, Jeremy Irons, Prince, Kate Winslet and Winona Ryder.

## The Individualist Levels

### Healthy

### Creativity

At his or her best, the healthy Individualist is a profoundly creative being. This creative stream flows strongly and freely, as they express their own personal feelings while at the same time inspiring others to connect with their own creativity and maybe even bring it to new levels. The healthy Four understands that what is personal is universal. She can transform any pain she might have experienced into gold, inspiring others in the process. This constant flow of creativity will enable the Individualist to self-renew and self-generate.

### Self-Awareness

The Four's innate tendency for self-reflection leads to a deep understanding of the self that they can also use for the service of others, helping them to understand their feelings and motivations also. They are intuitive, in touch with their inner impulses and sensitive to the extreme, but in a positive way. They help and deal with other people in a compassionate, tactful and gentle way.

**Individualism**

The clue is in the name! Here, the Four's strong sense of individualism is expressed in a healthy way. The Four at this stage of their development knows him or herself extremely well and is always true to this self. The Type Four at this level is emotionally honest to a fault and has no problem revealing his or her true self, due to the knowledge that the whole range of emotions is common to all. They understand that the courage to show and express vulnerability is actually a strength. Deeply humane, these people can be surprisingly funny, possessing a very ironic view of life. Those around them come to rely on their emotional strength.

**Neutral**

**Romanticism**

The Four at this level of maturity strives to create an aesthetically beautiful life for him or herself. This is because a gorgeous environment uplifts them and elevates their mood. This could manifest in a beautiful home with original artwork adorning the walls. Although the Four is not completely immune to image-consciousness, he or she is most concerned with choosing visual art that speaks to his or her soul. The Individualist or the Romantic at this level has a rich fantasy life and places a high value on passion and the imagination.

**Self-Absorption**

At a somewhat lower level, the tendency of Fours is to disappear too deeply into their own heads. They will internalize everything, becoming unhealthily introverted and overly moody. Here, the Individualist will be self-conscious and shy and will withdraw instead of dealing with their issues and bravely facing the world. They are hypersensitive and will go to great lengths to protect their self-image - essentially staying away from other people, whom they fear might too easily damage it.

**Self-Pity**

This tendency to go deeply within can descend into the Four living in a kind of fantasy world where they develop a sense of disdain for themselves and others. They can use this as an excuse to be self-indulgent in their emotions and habits and consequently go on to lead decadent and overly sensual lives. A healthy inclination towards daydreaming gets out of hand and they become increasingly unproductive and impractical. The Four might be envious of others at this level of maturity and this makes them even more melancholy.

**Unhealthy**

**Alienation**

Unhealthy fours experience alienation from both the self and others. Maybe they have been disappointed by dreams that have not come to fruition or people who have let them down. They will be very angry with themselves and this anger can turn inward and become depression. They feel blocked, both emotionally and creatively and this can expand into a feeling of paralysis. The sense of shame can be deep and all these negative emotions can leave the Four so exhausted that they can barely function.

**Self-Contempt**

The deeply unhealthy Four treats his or herself with contempt and believes absolutely that this is how other people view them too. They are tormented by desperate thoughts about their failings which sadly lead to feelings of self-hatred. The propensity to blame other people for all this pain results in the Four rejecting anyone who tries to help them.

**Despair**

A sense of hopelessness abounds and leads to self-destructive thoughts and behavior such as alcohol and drug abuse. Escaping profound pain is the aim here. At its absolute worst, the plight of the unhealthy Four is psychological breakdown or even suicide.

## The Individualist Wings

**Type Four with a Three Wing (4W3)**

Think creativity, curiosity and a lively intelligence. This variant of the Type Three personality has a multitude of ideas and knows how to use them. The rich fantasy life of the Four is married with the drive and capacity for action of the Three, resulting in dreams becoming reality and creative businesses that thrive.

The practicality of the Three balances out the Four's proclivity for drama and melancholy. The focus is very much on career and ambitious goals. The Three wing can give the Four more confidence and extroversion. It can draw the normally introverted Four into more social settings and they might actually be able to enjoy group activities! The Three also lends energy which leads the Fours out of their heads and into the world.

The flip side of this, when the negative aspects of the Four combine with the negative aspects of the Three, is a different story. Then this variant will struggle with shame. They will become obsessive about the image they are projecting and their relationships will be filled with every kind of drama. They may look for a sense of authenticity outside of themselves - where it never is. They will try all sorts of tactics to seek approval, growing angry and competitive in the process. They might even get into financial difficulties as they spend excessively in an effort to impress.

**Type Four With a Five Wing (4W5)**

The healthy strain of this fusion results in a wonderful blend of the heart and the mind. The Four's inclination to delve deeply into feelings is tempered by the Five's impartiality. This can allow the Individualist to view his or her life in a more objective way - facts are more likely to be brought into play. In addition, the Four's depth of feeling merged with the Five's brain energy creates someone who is both wise and empathetic.

The intellectual capacity of the Five wonderfully complements the profound insight of the Individualist. The Four with a Five wing is a deep, sensitive and perceptive in often ground-breaking ways. They are often quiet and introverted on the outside but there is a lot of activity going on within - both intellectually and emotionally.

When the mix doesn't go so well, the Four with a Five wing can become overwhelmed by out-of-control thoughts and emotions. Their inner life becomes so intense that it is almost unbearable for them. When sufficiently tortured, the 4W5 will withdraw from the world, including from those close to them, feeling painfully alone. Their relationships could suffer and so could their careers. Their inner world becomes their reality and they will reject all offers of help, because they find it hard to trust. They feel that the weight of the world is on their shoulders and can find it a challenge to even look after their own basic needs.

## Advice for The individualist

1. Order and discipline are not your natural enemies, especially when they are self-imposed. As a Type Four, you need a healthy dose of discipline to bring your inspired ideas out into the world, for instance, as artistic products or heart-centered businesses. Daydreaming will only get you so far. The world needs dreamers who make their dreams a reality!

2. Guard against your tendency towards self-indulgence, for example, when it comes to food, alcohol or drugs. You can help yourself by striving to maintain balance in your life, fostering healthy habits such as regular sleep, exercise and good nutrition.

3. Do not be a slave to your negative thought patterns. It is all too easy for Fours under stress to fall victim to the demons in their own heads. Find ways to distract yourself when you find yourself heading down a negative path - a favourite comedy show, uplifting music or a walk in

the beauty of nature are just some examples. Just don't let yourself go down this route. It is the equivalent of beating yourself up.

4. You are not your feelings. Feelings are of the moment. They are not fixed and they do not define your character - they are not who you are. There is no need to let them lead you astray as they can be very misleading.

5. Don't wait until you are ready to try something or do something. You might never feel ready - a Four seldom will! The trick is to do it scared. To plough on regardless, even if all the pieces do not yet appear to be in place. There is real power in making a start and you will be amazed at how things come together as you go. Just do it!

# Chapter Six - The Investigator (Type 5)

*Also known as the Observer or the Sage*

## Fifteen Signs You're An Investigator

1. You have an insatiable need to find out why things are the way they are - scientifically and otherwise.

2. You have a strong urge to question the status quo.

3. You feel that a day in which you haven't learned anything new is a day wasted.

4. If a subject or activity captures your interest, you focus your attention on it intently, until you have fully mastered it.

5. You might have been described by others - either to your face or otherwise! - as eccentric.

6. You hate being pressured into making quick decisions.

7. You are inclined to hold tension in your gut.

8. You might sometimes feel that you are "stuck" in your head and that it takes quite an effort to get back into your body.

9. You are not big on small talk. You find it uncomfortable and, quite frankly, a complete waste of time.

10. Your privacy is of the utmost importance to you and it is quite common for you to experience other people as intrusive.

11. You might feel the need to acquire knowledge and expertise in a bid to overcome deep-seated feelings of inadequacy and self-doubt.

12. You are highly likely to be an expert in your field and that field might be scholarly or highly technical.

13. You have a propensity to withdraw into the safety of your mind when life seems too threatening or overly demanding.

14. You are most probably well-read, not to mention thoughtful and intelligent.

15. It takes you a while to become comfortable with another person, but once you have achieved that level of comfort, you are a devoted companion and that friendship is likely to last a lifetime.

Do you think you might possibly be a Five?

## The Inspector Overview

The Investigator spends a lot of time in his or her own head. This is a similarity they have with the Four, but while the Four's comfort zone is in the realm of the imagination and the emotions, the five exists comfortably in the intellect. The Inspector has the habit of retreating into the world of thought when life gets too much. This is their safe place, where they can prepare to face the outside world once again because they like to be prepared and absolutely hate to be put on the spot. They are afraid, in fact, that they don't have what it takes to fully face life.

The Investigator, as the name implies, is sometimes scientifically oriented, but they may also strive for excellence in the area of the humanities.

The type Five can come across as eccentric. This might have something to do with their refusal to bend their beliefs to conform to the mainstream opinion. Freedom of thought is of paramount importance to the Observer, but they can be shy and struggle when it comes to dealing with and expressing their emotions. For this reason, relationships can be difficult for the type Five. This will make them feel lonely at times. Their independent nature can also add to the challenge of relationships, both in the romantic sense, but also when it comes to accepting help from well-meaning people.

The Investigator can be quite a sensitive soul. This makes them feel vulnerable so they commonly adopt coping mechanisms to shield themselves. This can make them come across as intellectually arrogant or carelessly indifferent. This also doesn't help with relationships! But if you learn how to penetrate these barriers, you've got yourself a friend for life.

Because of their need for privacy and fear of intrusion, Fives usually disguise their very strong feelings. This disguise can be extremely effective. For some Fives, one of their biggest fears is of being overwhelmed, so they attempt to keep their lives as simple as possible, making few demands on others in the hope that they will have few demands made on them in return.

Historical or famous Fives of note include: Albert Einstein, Stephen Hawking, Vincent Van Gogh, Georgia O'Keefe, Emily Dickinson, Bill Gates, Eckhart Tolle, Alfred Hitchcock, The Buddha, Oliver Sacks, Edvard Munch, Friedrich Nietzsche, James Joyce, Jean-Paul

Sartre, Stephen King, Salvador Dali, Agatha Christie, Mark Zuckerberg, Kurt Kobain, Peter Gabriel, Marlene Dietrich, Jodie Foster, Gary Larson, David Lynch, Tim Burton, Stanely Kubrick, Annie Liebovitz and Susan Sontag.

## The Investigator Levels

### Healthy

**Visionary**

The healthy Five is open-minded to the core. He or she can see the big picture while at the same time, appreciating and comprehending the minutiae. Their view of the world is visionary, seeing everything that can be improved for future generations and having some idea of how to make these improvements happen. They are the pioneers of the world; they are the scientists that make ground-breaking discoveries and the intellectuals that change the way we perceive the forces around us.

**Observant**

The healthy Five doesn't miss a thing. Their mental alertness is extraordinarily acute and their ability to focus and concentrate is second to none. They are perceptive and insightful with limitless curiosity. Their intellect is always seeking something new to sink its teeth into.

**Expert**

You will often find a five at the zenith of their chosen filed, as they have a seemingly unlimited capacity to attain mastery of whatever it is that interests them. They find knowledge wildly exciting and their passion often causes them to innovate and invent. Their work is often highly original and of great value to the world. The Investigator at this healthy level is frequently independent and possesses some marvellous idiosyncrasies.

**Neutral**

**Conceptualizing**

The Five will usually work everything out in their minds before acting on an idea. This allows them to fine tune everything from the outset. They love to be prepared and have all the required resources at their fingertips. They are studious and hard-working and often become specialists within their fields, while not being afraid to challenge the accepted way of doing things.

**Detached**

The Investigator, or the Observer, can sometimes become so involved in their intellectual world or the complex project on which they are working, that they become quite detached from reality. They lose touch with the real world, often in quite a disembodied way and become so preoccupied by their visions that matters such as relationships go by the wayside. At this point, the Five displays a kind of high-strung intensity and might even develop a fascination with offbeat or disturbing subjects.

**Antagonistic**

Beware of trying to interfere with the not-so-mature Five's interior world. They will not thank you for it! They will defend their personal vision at all costs, becoming aggressive and rude with those who oppose their - often radical - views.

## Unhealthy

### Reclusive

The shyness of an unhealthy Five can go into overdrive. Not only do they become isolated from other humans, but also from reality. Their eccentricity is no longer pleasant and their personality becomes increasingly unstable. They shun company and tend to live a hermit-like existence.

### Obsessive

This is obsession in its most unhealthy form. Their ideas become threatening - even to themselves. The Investigator in this state is delusional and suffers from phobias.

### Deranged

At the lowest possible level, we are in the area of schizotypal personality disorders. It is a dangerously self-destructive state and psychosis or suicide may be the end result.

# The Investigator Wings

### Type Five with a Four wing (5W4)

The influence of the Four wing on the Type Five personality can cause them to be more comfortable when it comes to expressing their emotions. They are still curious, reserved and perhaps a little more creative.

It should come as no surprise that the Type Five with a Four wing likes to be alone as both types in their purity enjoy alone time.

The strengths of the 5W4 include a capacity for deep attentiveness and the ability to observe and understand the most tiny details. They think and express themselves creatively and work well independently. But like everyone else, The Type Five with a Four wing is by no means perfect. He or she can be hyper-sensitive and also struggle, at times, to think in a practical and realistic way. They can be too self-absorbed and are prone to distancing themselves from other people.

If you need to communicate with an Investigator with a Five wing, you will do well to be as clear as possible and give them adequate time to process before pressing them for a response. If you are working with them, you would be advised to keep meetings to a minimum, be concise in your explanations and sensitive when giving feedback.

This variant of the Observer is energized by gaining knowledge, new skills and by being appreciated. They will feel drained if they have to spend too much time with other people or forced into situations that overwhelm them. And they certainly do not appreciate harsh criticism!

**Type Five with a Six wing (5W6)**

When the Six wing is dominant in the Type Five, the Investigator becomes more cooperative. Such a person will also be more inclined to use their impressive knowledge to solve problems rather than to intellectualize. This modification on the Five is inclined to be logical, independent and practical. They desire to be of use and to put their knowledge to work. They want to make the world a better place and feel more worthy in the process.

Their more positive traits include such qualities as focus and good organization, not to mention a passion for learning and improving. They often have a great capacity for solving complex problems and they are the type you want to have around in a crisis as they are adept at remaining calm.

However, the Type Five with a Six wing does have various blind spots. They can have difficulty relating to others and can be overly defensive in their wish to protect their privacy. They can come across as cold and aloof and need to be inspired in order to take any action.

This alternative Investigator loves to solve problems, especially when it makes them feel as if they are making a valuable contribution to society. Their pursuit of knowledge is enthusiastic, particularly when it comes to areas in which they are personally interested. They are drained by spending too much time around others and energized by spending time alone. Always be aware of their propensity for self-doubt in your dealings with them.

## Advice for The Investigator

1. Stay in your body. Your intellect is a wonderful tool but it is also necessary to stay connected to other people and to the real world. An excellent way of doing this is by staying in touch with your body and your physical sensations through exercise.

2. Trust is an issue for a Five and because of this, they can find it very hard to open up to other people. When they experience conflict in a relationship, their natural tendency is to withdraw and isolate themselves. This is, of course, not particularly healthy behavior. The Investigator would do well to remember that conflicts are a normal

part of every relationship and the appropriate course of action is to work things out.

3. It is tough for Type Five on The Enneagram to relax. This is because of their innate intensity. It is therefore important for the Five to devise ways to wind down that are suitable and appropriate. Meditation, yoga and running are all recommended.

4. The Five can lose his or her sense of perspective and quite easily feel overwhelmed as there are so many factors to consider! To help you make an accurate assessment in these circumstances, seek out the advice of someone you trust (after first working on your trust issues)!

5. Be selective in the projects you choose to become involved with. Make sure that they are life-affirming and take you in the direction in which you want to go. Make sure you are not distracting yourself in an unworthy way and wasting your precious time.

# Chapter Seven - The Loyalist (Type 6)

*Also known as the Loyal Skeptic or the Traditionalist*

## Fifteen Signs You're A Loyalist

1. You hang on to toxic friendships and situations longer than you should.

2. You are perceived - and quite rightly so - as a good trouble-shooter. This is because you are excellent at anticipating problems and devising appropriate solutions.

3. You can hold a lot of tension in the area around your diaphragm.

4. You worry a lot. Let's face it, there are so many things that can go wrong!

5. You are loyal to ideas and belief systems as well as to your friends and family members.

6. You can have trouble connecting with your own inner guidance system. This can cause you to lack confidence in your own judgment.

7. A sense of security is of the utmost importance to you and finding and holding on to this security is a driving force.

8. You tend to ask for advice from many different people before making a decision. As you mature, however, the amount of people upon whose opinion you rely may lessen.

9. You are contradictory in nature and your personality contains many opposites. This is because you tend to go back and forth between various different influences. To paraphrase Walt Whitman - you are large, you contain multitudes!

10. The people around you know that you are reliable and that they can depend on you. You are always there for them.

11. You appreciate order. It is important for you to have a firm structure in place, to have double-checked all your facts and to have a back-up plan.

12. Peace of mind can be elusive for you.

13. You can be suspicious of other people and authorities. You wait until the person or organization has proven themselves fully before giving them your trust.

14. You might have a tendency to act defiantly against whatever it is that you find threatening. In this instance, you may become a rebel and challenge authority.

15. You are responsible, hard-working and trustworthy. Those who are lucky enough to have your friendship know that you will always have their backs.

Did you say "that could be me" more than a few times? If so, read on. You could be a Loyalist!

## The Loyalist Overview

As a typical Six, you crave security above all else. This is because you wrestle with a deep-rooted sense of anxiety which is at the core of your being, whether you are aware of it or not.

Type Six on The Enneagram tends to worry a lot. They have no problem imagining all sorts of scenarios, far-fetched or otherwise, in which everything goes wrong. They fear that there is nothing steady enough to hold on to, so they attempt to create such steadiness for themselves, often in personal relationships.

Their propensity to imagine every single possible disastrous outcome makes the Type Six an excellent trouble-shooter, and therefore very useful for others to have around. But this is not much of a comfort for the Loyalist, who struggles to find peace of mind with this constant focus on potential problems.

This can also have the effect of causing the Six to lack spontaneity. Because how can they possibly carry out an action without meticulous planning first? If they don't do this, won't everything collapse like a house of cards?

This is a lot of anxiety to live with. It also makes the Six more suspicious than the average person. You really have to prove yourself to win the Loyalist's trust. But once you succeed in doing so, you have a steadfast friend for life. Loyalty is a fantastic trait, but the Six would do well to make sure they are not staying loyal to someone or something long after it is time to move on from them.

The Six often has a complicated relationship with authority. On the one hand, their desire to have someone or something to believe in might cause them to give their control over to an external force. On the other hand, they also have the propensity to distrust and be suspicious of authority. How confusing! Sometimes a Six individual will lean further in one direction than the other. Sometimes, they might go back and forth between these two different attitudes.

The Loyalist also has two different strategies when it comes to coping with fear. One strategy is phobic, which will cause them to be compliant and cooperative. The other is counter-phobic, which means that the Six will take a defiant stand against anything they find threatening. Rebelliousness and aggression can be the hallmark here.

There have been countless noteworthy Loyalists. Here are a number of them: Sigmund Freud, Robert F. Kennedy, Malcolm X, Diana, Princess of Wales, U2's Bono, Julia Roberts, Ellen Degeneres, Spike Lee, Krishnamurti, Edgar Hoover, George H.W. Bush, J.R.R. Tolkein, Melissa Etheridge, Bruce Springsteen, Mike Tyson, Woody Allen, Sally Field, David Letterman, Newt Gingrich, Jay Leno, Katie Holmes, Benn Affleck, Tom Hanks, Mel Gibson, Diane Keaton, Mark Wahlberg, Dustin Hoffman, Oliver Stone, Michael Moore, John Grisham, Prince Harry, Robert F. Kennedy, Mark Twain and Richard Nixon.

## The Loyalist Levels

**Healthy**

**Trusting**

This trust is for the self yet it also extends to others. The healthy Six has got the balance right, maintaining their independence while at the same time achieving a cooperative interdependence with others. They are able to collaborate with others and work together in harmony. When the Six learns to believe in herself, she can act with courage and positivity, making her a fabulous leader. She will also be richly self-expressive.

**Appealing to Others**

When the Six is fully mature and gets her or himself together, they can be a most endearing and lovable type. People react strongly to them in a very positive way and have a genuine affection for them, which they are likely to receive back in kind. Once they have their trust issues sorted out, the healthy Six successfully blends with others, leading to fruitful friendships and alliances.

**Dedicated**

When the healthy Loyalist finds a movement or an individual in which they fully believe, there is no one who is more dedicated. They will build communities, sacrifice for others or for a greater cause, and bring cooperation, security and stability wherever they go. They are determined, reliable, trustworthy and responsible.

**Neutral**

**Safe**

At this neutral level, a kind of contraction occurs and the Loyalist has more of a tendency to play it safe. This is not always a terrible thing. At this point of their development, the Six invests their energy in whatever seems likely to remain stable and secure. They organize and create structure and look to authorities that can promise a sense of continuity. They never let up in anticipating what can go wrong and trying to put systems in place to prevent such problems occurring.

**Indecisive**

If the Six in neutral mode feels confused or that too many demands are being made on him or her, they will give off many contradictory signals. They will procrastinate and become overly cautious, indecisive and evasive. They will be increasingly negative as their anxiety levels rise and unpredictability results. They may even react in passive-aggressive ways.

**Reactive**

The fear takes over the Six, although they may not consciously be aware of this. Instead, they blame other people for their uncomfortable feelings, taking it out on the "outsider," for instance. They will be defensive at this level and highly sensitive to threats, constantly monitoring others to work out whether they are a friend or foe. They can be authoritarian and suspicious of everyone and their manner can become belligerent.

**Unhealthy**

**Panicked**

Fear takes over at this unhealthy stage. This highly insecure feeling causes the Six to panic and become extremely volatile. They look for increasingly strong authority figures and institutions in order to buoy up their own acute feelings of inferiority and defenselessness. They will be extremely critical and difficult to be around.

**Persecuted**

This all-pervasive feeling that others are out to get them can make the unhealthy Six lash out irrationally which, in the worst case scenario, can lead to violence.

**Hysterical**

This is the lowest a Six can go. It is a self-destructive level where alcohol and drugs might be abused. It is the realm of the Paranoid Personality Disorders and they might even attempt to take their own lives.

# The Loyalist Wings

**Type Six with a Five wing (6W5)**

For the most part, the Type Six with a Five wing is a traditional sort, conservative in their views and desirous of fitting into a trustworthy group. Safety is the name of the game here. Although the Six desire to feel secure is colored by the Five need to analyze things right down to their component parts.

When well-balanced, the 6W5 is able to let go of anxiety. This makes them good-humored, relaxed and endearing. They finally feel that they can trust life and in turn, this is a person that can be trusted and relied upon one-hundred-percent.

It is lovely to have the balanced Type Six with a Five wing as a family member. Possessing a quiet confidence, they will be a wonderful companion and source of wisdom. You will be able to develop a deep bond with this type and the Five wing will add a perceptiveness to their enduring friendship.

But imbalance can sometimes ensue and anxiety can rear its ugly head again. They look for a reason for this rising tension and if one is not easily forthcoming, they will find someone to blame for it!

If stress levels increase, the world becomes an increasingly threatening place for the 6W5 and paranoia can begin to set in. They might feel that everybody is out to get them and in this desperately uncomfortable place of tension, they might look for somebody to come to their rescue.

Sixes want to be likable and attractive to others, but Five does not really know how to achieve this. Their attire tends not to be overly showy or flashy.

It may suit the Loyalist with a Five wing to find employment that combines being part of a group with being alone. A forest ranger or a bus driver might be an example of this. Some become involved in risky protection activities such as fire-fighting and others might look for ways to advocate for under privileged people.

**The Type Six with a Seven wing (6W7)**

The Type Six with a Seven wing is a lot less subdued than the Type Six with a Five wing. Their reactions are more impulsive and colourful and they are less likely to analyze a situation, instead jumping in with both feet. However, the caution of the Six will usually pull back the flamboyance of the Seven before it gets too out-of-hand.

There is a back and forth here between flamboyance and caution which can cause some emotional volatility.

At its best, the Loyalist with a Seven wing is steady, calm and deliberate. When in balance, both the Six's anxiety and the Seven's impulsiveness tend to diminish. They still love having fun with their friends but the desperate drive for security is transformed into an inner strength. They make great parents or siblings.

The 6W7 frequently develops a strong spiritual side, experiencing a deep sense of belonging with the universe. Their faith is a great source of comfort to them.

Of course, things can get out of kilter. If the Type Six with a Seven wing gets out of whack, anxiety and insecurity come to the fore once more. Here, they will jump from one extreme emotional state to the other, desperately searching for someone to help them and feeling increasing despair.

In a more stressed state, the 6W7 can come across as clingy and desperate and this drives other people away. They get themselves into all sorts of trouble as they feel increasingly dependent and tense.

This variant of the Six is often physically attractive and appealing to the opposite sex. In terms of the world of work, they may look to fun professions which also have an element of security inherent in them such as cartoonists or movie reviewers.

## Advice for The Loyalist

1. Trust is an issue for you. If you are honest with yourself, you can most probably identify a few people in your life that you can trust completely. Cherish these people and hold them dear. Let them know how much you appreciate them, even though this might make you feel vulnerable. If you genuinely do not have anyone in your life that you feel you can trust, make it a point to find someone, believing that there are trustworthy people out there. You may have to move past your fears to do so, but the end result will be worth it.

2. The Type Six can sometimes use projection as a defense mechanism, in other words, attributing to others what you cannot accept in yourself. This hardly seems fair, does it? Watch out for your tendency to resort to this behaviour. Do not blame others for things that you yourself have done or brought upon yourself in some way. You become your own worst enemy when you become negative and self-doubting, causing even more harm to yourself than you do to others.

3. Do all you can to quell your anxiety. A key step might be to just accept that this is part of your nature and also to acknowledge that more people suffer from anxiety than you probably realize. Try to relax. Everything is going to be fine!

4. Other people like you more than you think they do. That's something else to stop worrying about!

5. Try not to overreact when you are under stress. This involves managing your own thoughts more effectively and acknowledging that most of what you have wasted your time worrying about has never arisen. Fearful thoughts have no purpose but to weaken your ability to act and make things better.

# Chapter Eight - The Enthusiast (Type 7)

*Also known as the Epicure*

## Fifteen Signs You're an Enthusiast

1. You are very curious and always looking for new experiences to prevent boredom from creeping in!

2. You are wonderfully optimistic and enthusiastic, something other people often find "catching" and love to be around.

3. You don't store as much tension in your body as other types and tend to be loose and flexible. The challenge for you is to stay grounded.

4. You are not really concerned with the image you project and are more interested in having fun and doing your own thing.

5. Other people accuse you of being restless and may comment that you have trouble settling down to one thing.

6. You see life as an exciting adventure, with something better always around the corner.

7. You are probably an extrovert and great at networking.

8. You don't believe in denying yourself anything - you want to experience all the pleasures that life has to offer.

9. You seek distraction from internal negativity in the external world, for example, by keeping really busy and making sure you are stimulated at all times.

10. You have above average or high self-esteem, believing in your strengths and your talents.

11. You are versatile and can often be multi-talented. Highly practical, you can be engaged in many projects at once.

12. You are most probably intelligent with an agile mind, but not necessarily studious or intellectual.

13. You may have brilliant mind-body co-ordination and manual dexterity.

14. You are naturally good-humored and cheerful, and normally do not take yourself too seriously.

15. You have an over-arching desire to live life to the fullest!

Did you recognize yourself in the above signs? Were you proud? Read on and find out if this is your Type.

## The Enthusiast Overview

# Enneagram

As far as the Enthusiast is concerned, life is meant to be one big, exciting adventure from start to finish. This makes them fun to be around and people are naturally attracted to their *joie de vivre*. They are always looking to the future and looking forward to something better that's around the next corner.

Most Sevens are extroverted. They have tons of energy which they like to expend in all sorts of ways, being multi-talented and creative. Indeed, they are highly practical with multiple skills and may possess an entrepreneurial spirit. If they do have a flaw in this regard, it is that they sometimes have difficulty focusing. Also, they have so many interests and such high hopes for the "next big thing" that they can find it hard to settle on just one project and bring it fully to fruition. They will, however, be adept at promoting themselves and their product, business or service and they are natural networkers.

Sevens do not believe in denying themselves and they can be compulsive pleasure seekers. They sometimes use this activity to distract themselves from anything negative that might be going on in their lives. This may lead to a tendency towards addiction - drugs, gambling, etc.

The typical Enthusiast, or Epicure, as he or she is also known, is usually not lacking in confidence. While this is healthy, this can at times veer towards being self-centered or having an inflated sense of entitlement.

The Seven does not always like confronting the harsh realities of life and other people's problems, but if they run away from confronting such emotions, they run the risk of storing up problems for themselves and suffering from anxiety or depression down the road.

Of course, there have been loads of famous Sevens. Some you have most probably heard of are: The Dalai Lama, Mozart, John F. Kennedy, Richard Branson, Bette Midler, Goldie Hawn, Robin Williams, Galileo Galilei, Thomas Jefferson, Amelia Earhart,

Kandinsky, Noel Coward, Joe Biden, Silvio Berlusconi, Suze Orman, Elton John, Fred Astaire, Joan Rivers, George Clooney, Jim Carrey, Leonardo DiCaprio, Cameron Diaz, Simon Cowell, Larry King, Howard Stern, David Duchovny, Robert Downey Junior, Brad Pitt, Cary Grant, Stephen Spielberg, Russell Brand, Miley Cyrus, Sacha Baron Cohen and Sarah Palin.

## The Enthusiast Levels

### Healthy

### Joyful

The Enthusiast at his highest level is all gratitude and appreciation for everything he has, including all the simple pleasures in life. This ability to assimilate experiences in an in-depth way leads to a kind of ecstasy that borders on the spiritual.

### Enthusiastic

Well, it is their name! This extroverted type is good-humored, lively and spontaneous. They respond to everything in an excitable and eager way, finding even "normal" life experiences quite invigorating.

### Multi-talented

Their many gifts make them accomplished and productive - well able to achieve in lots of different areas. Due to their enthusiasm for a broad range of subjects, they can often be compelled to develop a variety of skills.

## Neutral

### Restless

So many choices, so little time - this could be the mantra of the average Enthusiast. They have a fear of missing out which makes it difficult for them to choose between one option and another. Focus can be difficult to achieve as they are constantly seeking out new adventures. They can be sophisticates at this stage in their maturity. They like variety, plenty of cash and keeping up with the latest fashion.

### Hyperactive

The fear of being bored keeps the Seven at this level in constant motion. They don't know what they need to feel satisfied so they throw themselves into perpetual activity. They will perform and exaggerate and behave in more and more flamboyant ways. They will find it difficult to follow through on their ideas.

### Consuming

They never feel that they have enough. They consume to excess, whether that be shopping, food or drugs. They are never satisfied, no matter what, and this can lead them to be demanding and hardened.

## Unhealthy

### Addicted

The unhealthy Seven does not know when to stop. They cannot control their impulses and so desperate are they to soothe their anxiety. They can sink to levels of depravity and their behavior may become abusive and offensive.

**Out of Control**

From bad to worse! In a desperate bid for escapism, these Sevens are incapable of dealing with anxiety properly and may descend into erratic or impulsive actions.

**Self-Destructive**

The lowest possible level for the Seven to sink to. They have probably ruined their health at this point and given up on themselves and life. They're most likely deeply depressed and may attempt suicide. Their symptoms here would not be dissimilar to bipolar disorder.

# The Enthusiast Wings

**The Seven with a Six wing (7W6)**

The hallmarks of a Seven with a Six wing are that they are enthusiastic and adventurous - as you would expect with a seven - but with a healthy dose of responsibility thrown into the mix. Sounds like quite a good balance, doesn't it? They still love to pursue new experiences but they are much better able to stick to prior commitments.

Although this all sound perfect, there is a potential downside too: a Fear of Missing Out (FOMO)! The Seven with a Six wing really wants to honor their commitments, but what if a wonderful last minute opportunity arises? You can see how this variant of the number Seven is likely to feel torn. They want, most of all, to feel happy and fulfilled and the way the Seven goes about this is by finding joy in even the smallest of experiences. But the Seven with a Six wing might have a tendency to rationalize away negative feelings, unconsciously convincing themselves of their own happiness when this is, in fact, not the case.

They will go to great lengths to avoid being upset - even rationalizing and justifying the bad behavior of others, because they value happiness and optimism above all else. Relationships are very important to them, as is pleasure-seeking on all levels and this all abiding fear of missing out on potential opportunities.

The Enthusiast with a Six wing has many positive traits. The inclination is to be highly productive. They also cooperate well with others, whether they are fellow workers, clients or other collaborators. They manage to remain sensitive to the feelings of others, not riding roughshod over their emotions in the pursuit of their own goals and happiness. Even when confronted with a stressful situation, the Seven's optimism will pull them through and allow them to remain buoyant. They are quick thinkers but do not merely consider the surface issues. They are capable of going deep and considering matters in a thorough way.

But, of course, we all have our blind spots to contend with and this variant of the Type Seven is no exception to that rule. Unlike the "pure" Type Seven, the Seven with a Six wing cares deeply about what other people think of them and is easily affected by their opinions. This might cause them to doubt themselves and lead to a feeling of all-pervading anxiety. And the Seven's propensity to become bored does not go away. They may easily become restless in a job or a relationship and crave something new. And when stress hits, the Enthusiast with a Six wing could struggle with organization and focus.

When dealing with an Enthusiast with this wing, you will do well to remain optimistic and upbeat and to really listen to them, taking all their ideas seriously. They love to chat in a free-flowing, light-hearted way and they also greatly appreciate encouragement and support. This will especially be the case when they are expressing difficult emotions, which they find challenging.

Remember how much they are energized by new ideas and experiences and how creativity inspires them. They love meeting new people and going to places where there are large gatherings of folk to get to know. Take your 7W6 to a party or a concert. They will love you for it!

What they do not thrive on is overly rigid schedules or rules. Do not beat them down with negativity and make sure that the Seven with a Six wing in your life has plenty of company to keep them happy and energized. They absolutely hate routine and thrive on lots of interesting choices - not to mention the freedom to make such choices.

In summary, the Enthusiast with a Six wing is a curious type and can be wildly productive given the right circumstances. Although they still seek new experiences, they are steadfastly loyal to friends and family. Creative and adventurous, they also love to build a sense of community. They are sometimes known as "The Pathfinder."

**Type Seven with an Eight wing (7W8)**

The Eight wing lends a toughness to the Type Seven. It also inclines them to be more work-oriented. They are still enthusiastic - as the main hallmark of umber Seven on The Enneagram - but they have an added determination.

In a general sense, there is still a fear of missing out, but this manifests itself more in a fear of deprivation rather that a fear of missing out on excitement. The pursuit of new opportunities is still a high priority and so is the dislike of rigidity and scheduling. The Seven's basic desire to be happy and fulfilled is tempered somewhat by the Eight wing and can now be more accurately described as a wanting to be satisfied and content.

Although they still love to be out in the world, going to events where there are lots of people, such as big parties and festivals and also travelling to exotic places, the Eight wing gives a more protectionist dimension to the Seven's actions and they defend themselves by justifying the poor behavior of others and by rationalizing away their own bad feelings.

Optimism is still a top priority for the Seven with an Eight wing, as is personal gratification. They are always on the lookout for new opportunities and consider it highly important to be open to new experiences. Fear of missing out does not go away with the presence of the Eight wing. They still crave and adore the company of other humans and will justify the negative actions of such humans to prevent themselves from feeling bad.

This variant of the Seven wing has many attributes. They have a knack for remaining positive, no matter what, and staying in that all-important high energy mindset. Self-confidence comes to them easily and they often have a natural charisma that attracts other people like bees around a honey pot. They are no shrinking violets either, and are able to stand up for and assert themselves. They are a good sort to have around you in a crisis, as they have the ability to remain calm in situations where many people are in a panic.

Like everyone else, however, the Enthusiast with an Eight wing has weaknesses that they must strive to overcome. The Eight wing does make the all-encompassing charm of the number Seven slightly less pervasive. Because of this, the Seven with an Eight wing can come across as quite blunt at times. They may offend people without realizing or without meaning to do so. They can also be impatient with situations and people. The Enthusiast with an Eight wing might be accused of focusing too much on their career and to the detriment of other aspects of their lives such as their relationships. They might be overly materialistic also, forgetting what is truly important in life. In spite of all this, they could still suffer from the Type Seven tendency to have difficulty following through on plans, once the initial enthusiasm has worn off.

When you are communicating with this alternative to the Type Seven, they will really appreciate it if you listen carefully to them. This is because they love to have conversations and expressing themselves is very important to them. They like their conversations to have a purpose, not just to wander aimlessly and their preference is to keep things upbeat. They want to get right to the point while also having the opportunity to share every single thought and idea that is going on inside their heads. They appreciate people being direct and honest with them and will happily cooperate to reach a compromise if an argument arises.

If you have a Seven with an Eight wing in your life, never lose sight that they love new experiences, especially fun occasions such as parties and celebrations, concerts and festivals and travelling to new and far flung destinations. Relationships are a big priority for them and you will get on better with your 7W6 if you allow them to be the center of attention from time to time! And they dearly love a good goal to accomplish.

Do not cut off their energy with rigid rules and limits. They hate, above all, to feel controlled. They also thrive on company - so why not give them yours?

The Type Seven with an Eight wing is sometimes known as the Opportunist.

## Advice for The Enthusiast

1. You love to have conversations and express all your many varied opinions, but be honest with yourself. Are you *really* listening to those with whom you are having conversations?
Active listening is an art worth cultivating. Think of all the new and interesting things you'll discover if you really take in what other people are saying to you. It might even lead to new opportunities. And there doesn't always have to be chatter. Silence is golden. Do not be afraid to put down your phone or turn off the TV. There are real and lasting benefits to be had from not distracting yourself all the time and staying present with your thoughts and emotions. Living with less external stimulation in this way, will help you to trust yourself. You might even be more satisfied when you start doing less. Now doesn't that sound like a huge relief?

2. Life is long and you don't have to experience everything all in one go. Imagine having every dinner you were ever going to eat all in one day! You would not want that. So that tempting car or cake, for instance, will still be in the show room or the shop next week – there may even be a better alternative. Let go of your compulsive fear of missing out on opportunities. They will come around again and you will be better able to judge which ones are really meant for you.

3. As a typical Seven, you would be well advised to observe your impulses instead of diving in head first. Do not give into them straight away, no matter how much you might want to do so. Instead, learn to judge which ones are worthy of acting upon. Not all impulses are created equally! As you become more observant and a better judge of all your different impulses, you will learn which ones are worth your focus, time and energy, and you can start living your life in a more beneficial way.

4. Experience is not all about quantity. It is about quality too. In other words, a few wonderful and deeply felt experiences can be better than a thousand scattered ones where you do not really allow yourself to be present. Good advice for the Seven is to stay in the moment and pay attention to what you are actually doing in the now, instead of constantly anticipating potentially better experiences. The latter is not the path to true satisfaction.

5. Question your desires. Is what you want really what you want? When you consider the likely long-term consequences of your current desires, do you still think you're longing for the right thing for you? Or will it only lead to disappointment or even unhappiness in the long run? Practice discernment at all times.

# Chapter Nine - The Challenger (Type 8)

*Also known as the Ruler*

## Fifteen Signs You're a Challenger

1. You like to be in charge. And why on earth *wouldn't* anyone put you in charge of things?

2. You hate, hate, hate to be controlled. In fact, you rarely let this happen to you and anyone who tries is met with a lot of attitude.

3. Others might accuse you of being domineering.

4. You have the capacity to work extremely hard in order to manifest your goals.

5. You are an excellent mentor and can effectively show others how to achieve as you have done, thus nurturing the leaders of the future.

6. You have a propensity for getting bored very quickly. This can also lead to impatience.

7. You can come across as somewhat fierce and others can find you intimidating at times.

8. Anger can be an issue for you and you are inclined to lose your temper fairly easily. Some people find this scary!

# Enneagram

9. As the name of this type implies, you love to take on a challenge and indeed, enjoy giving other people challenges too, thereby helping them to stretch their abilities and even to exceed themselves.

10. You have an in-built charisma or magnetism. This makes you an effective leader, no matter what sphere you live and work in. You can quite easily persuade others to follow you.

11. You have great energy and you use this - together with your formidable willpower - to leave your mark on society

12. You value independence highly and you are not afraid to stand alone, defying social convention if necessary.

13. You possess a steely determination which others find amazing and sometimes even logic-defying.

14. You have a powerful 'can do' attitude and tend to be extremely resourceful. You get things done, in a commanding way.

15. You have an abundance of common sense and this can greatly benefit those around you.

So what do you think? Are you a Challenger? Other people can offer their opinions but only you know for sure.

## The Challenger Overview

Control is at the heart of the Challenger's personality. At their core, they are totally unwilling to be controlled, whether it be by a person or by circumstances. It is of the utmost importance to an Eight that they remain the masters of their fates and the captains of their souls. The flip side of this is that they are inclined to be domineering. This coupled with their unwillingness to be controlled may lead them to try to control others. Ironic, is it not? A healthy Challenger is well able to keep this tendency under control but it is something that always has to be guarded against, especially as one moves down the maturity scale. It can be a recurring issue in the interpersonal relationships of an Eight.

Eights take the concept of being strong-willed to new heights. They are tough-minded to a fault and their enormous energy and practical nature aids them significantly in getting their own way.

The Challenger desires to get the most out of life and this can often extend to their physical appetites. They indulge in those appetites without experiencing a hint of unhealthy remorse.

Financial independence is a massive priority for the Challenger. He or she may have difficulty having a boss. They do know best, after all! Challengers tend to benefit from working in a field where they can be their own boss. Under certain circumstances, an Eight may feel the need to opt out of society altogether, finding other ways to gain financial freedom instead, as they are usually uncomfortable with hierarchies.

The Challenger has a deep and abiding fear of feeling vulnerable. This can be detrimental to their capacity to form intimate relationships because, obviously, intimacy requires vulnerability. Defenses need to be lowered! Of course, this involves letting go of the need to be in control and trust is of the greatest importance in this arena. Betrayal of any kind will cut the challenger to the quick. Woe betide the person who violates an Eight in this way!

Believe it or not, Eights can be sentimental. They hide it well, even from those closest to them, but it's true. This is an indication of how much the Eight fears being vulnerable. However, if you do manage to win their trust, you will have someone who stands by you no matter what. The Challenger is hugely protective of those in their inner circle - family and friends especially - and they will move mountains to provide for these people.

A big Achilles Heel for the Eight is their anger. At lower levels of maturity, this emotion can spiral out of control and turn into rage. Such aggression can even turn into violence and unhealthy Eights can be intimidating, ruthless and even dangerous.

Not surprisingly, there are many Eights who have achieved remarkable feats of success in this life. Some examples of these include: Winston Churchill, Oskar Schindler, Martin Luther King, Serena Williams, Barbara Walters, Toni Morrison, Frank Sinatra, Bette Davis, Paul Newman, Richard Wagner, Franklin D. Roosevelt, Fidel Castro, Lyndon Johnson, Golda Meir, Saddam Hussein, Donald Trump, Ernest Hemingway, James Brown, Queen Latifah, Aretha Franklin, Pink, Jack Black, Sean Connery, John Wayne, Mae West, Humphrey Bogart, Jack Black, Dr Phil, Roseanne Barr, Jack Nicholson, Tommy Lee Jones, Clint Eastwood, Lauren Bacall, Chrissie Hynde, Courtney Love, Pablo Picasso, Norman Mailer, Senator John McCain and last but not least, Indira Gandhi.

## The Challenger Levels

**Healthy**

**Heroism**

Not unlike Type One on the Enneagram, Type Eight possesses the qualities that heroes are made of. There is the potential here to climb awesome heights and to achieve historical greatness. At the peak of his or her health and maturity, an Eight can restrain their lesser impulses and become a truly magnanimous individual, attaining true self-mastery. Possessing massive courage, they are willing to face real danger in order to achieve their vision and make a true difference.

**Strong**

This strength comes with a remarkable self-confidence and self-assertiveness. They have no problem standing up for their needs and wants. The Eight at this healthy stage is full of drive and passion and no one is more resourceful than them. A 'can do' attitude is dominant in these types.

**Authoritative**

The natural leader or commander. The Eight will be the one who is not afraid to take the initiative to get things done and make things happen. Decision-making comes easily to them as they rarely doubt their own judgment. They are the people's champion. They will provide and protect and carry those who lack their strength. They are truly honourable.

**Neutral**

**Self-sufficient**

It is of utmost importance to the Challenger, at this stage of their development, that they have adequate resources, financially and otherwise. To this end, they will become profoundly pragmatic and enterprising. They will be the quintessential 'wheeler-dealer,' willing to deny even their own emotional needs as they take any necessary risks and put their noses to the grindstone.

## Domineering

At this not-so-mature level, the Challenger will seek to bend others' wills to their own. They have no compunction about imposing their vision on everyone else. Dominating other people, and equally their environment, the Eight will become a 'show off' and overly forceful. They do not appreciate anybody who has the temerity to question their word or their decisions and they must feel that people are supporting their efforts. They become egocentric at this point and forget to treat other individuals with the respect that they want and deserve.

## Intimidating

Matters go from bad to worse - for Eights and those around them - as we travel further down the maturity ladder. This is where the Challenger becomes more than challenging - they become adversarial, belligerent and confrontational. They will refuse to back down, even if they secretly suspect that they are wrong. This would be tantamount to losing face and they cannot allow that to happen! They will threaten and impose punishments in order to extract obedience from those around them, who at this stage are feeling increasingly insecure. They are their own worst enemies however, as their attitude and actions may well backfire, turning people against them and perhaps even causing them to join together against the Eight.

## Unhealthy

### Ruthless

At this immature level of development, things start to get quite nasty. Here the Eight will stop at nothing to get their own way including immoral behaviour and violence. If they are in a position to get away with being dictatorial, then they certainly will! They might resort to criminal behaviour, not caring if they rip people off. They will defy all attempts to control them.

### Delusional

Oh dear! At this stage of bad emotional health, the Eight will think that he or she is invincible. Their antics will now border on megalomania and extreme recklessness will be the order of the day. They believe they are truly invulnerable.

### Vengeful

"Never surrender!" will be their battle-cry, but not in a good way. At the lowest of the low, the Challenger will destroy everything and everyone that does not bend to their will. They will descend to all sorts of barbaric conduct, even murder. We are in the territory here of the sociopath.

## The Challenger Wings

### The Eight with a Seven wing (8W7)

A person doesn't get any tougher than the Type Eight with a Seven wing. They might even look tough, with broad, rough features and an enormous, muscular physique. And their actions might well match their appearance. This is because the Challenger with a Seven wing has so much powerful energy coursing through their system. The Eight's overpowering personality tends to dominate quite a bit and values being in charge above all else, including the Seven's need to be the life and soul of the party.

Their mode of appearance can vary wildly. When they are in the mood and the circumstances are right, they might be very well dressed and 'pulled together.' But at other times, when they are preoccupied, they might not be bothered at all about what they look like.

Of course, every single personality has the capacity to shine and the Eight with a Seven wing is no exception to this. When they're well-balanced, an 8W7 can be charming and tactful. If they have a sense of self-awareness, this can make them less aggressive and less extreme in their conduct. They realize that real power comes from within and that they do not have to put on a show of strength. They discover patience and learn to calm their more destructive impulses.

At their peak, the Challenger with a Seven wing will choose kindness instead of being argumentative. Picture a gentle giant. They will use their power for good, becoming considerate and perceptive in their dealings with people. They get in touch with their intuition and this allows them to accurately judge various situations. The highly integrated 8W7 has options available to him or her which are not possible at a lower level.

But with the good comes the bad. The Challenger with a Seven wing can actually be a physical danger to others. Insensitive, unsociable, with no regard for the rules that govern a civilized society, the 8W7 becomes a very rough character indeed. Think, here, of the quintessential bully or thug.

With even less integration, this variant of the Eight will lash out violently. He or she will be judgmental, defensive and intolerant. Their mantra is 'kill or be killed.'

In terms of professions that suit this type of Eight, they may include things like construction foreman, army general, or boxer. Of course, they can also be a stay-at-home mother! It is all possible.

**The Eight with a Nine wing (8W9)**

Physical power is still a huge component when it comes to the Challenger with a Nine wing. But Type Nine on The Enneagram has a passive quality causing this particular personality to be quiet but aggressive when provoked. Imagine a bear, normally slow-moving but capable of sudden violence. Eruptions of anger are possible. They usually move around quite slowly but they must feel that the situation is under control before they can relax.

When well-balanced, this variant of the Eight is a joy to be around. They will be kind and gentle and in touch with their inner guidance. They will not feel the need to dominate. Neither will they feel an impulse to withdraw. They wield their power wisely, knowing when it is of benefit to themselves and others to do so, and sensing when it is not.

At the very top level, the 8W9 possesses a powerful benevolence and has the capacity to be a great leader or teacher. They are tough when it is needed and gentle when that is what is required.

But when unhealthy, the Eight with a Nine wing develops a deep conflict within and becomes unpredictable and dangerous to be around. When they are quiet, you can be sure that there is anger lurking just beneath the surface. This can result in frequent explosions of rage.

At their worst, they can descend into a state of paranoid isolation. Intrude and you might be attacked or killed by this antisocial being who lacks compassion or conscience.

The Challenger with a Nine wing will normally not care about what they look like. They would rather just relax. They prefer jobs that mean they will not be overly bothered by other people. A truck driver or a night guard might be a good example. Of course, as with any type, you can find them anywhere!

## Advice for The Challenger

1. It is absolutely the case that you value your independence and this is not necessarily a bad thing. However, people need people, whether you like it or not and it is going to be necessary for you to let others in. It is not possible to function in this world as an island and people are not as expendable as you think they are. For example, you might need employees who are loyal and that you can trust. If you alienate them, you will lose them. Similarly, in your personal life, you will be isolated and lonely unless you let people in.

2. Choose your battles wisely! You don't have to win every battle and every argument. Let others have their way from time to time. It is not true power to 'beat' other people all the time. If you feel the need to dominate, it means that your ego is out of control and this will just lead to more unhealthy conflict. Avoid this.

3. Realize your true gifts and capacities, and use your power for good. Restrain yourself if you can foresee that your actions are likely to hurt others. Your real power is to motivate, uplift and to show others what they, too, are capable of. In this way, you can be of great service to others, perhaps helping them in a crisis. This is absolutely the way to inspire loyalty from people.

4. Another quick word about power: those who are attracted to you because of your power and because of this alone, have no real affection for you. They might just be using you as you use them back. Is this really how you want to live your life?

5. People are nicer than you think. So let them in, knowing that this is a sign of true strength and not weakness. When you are mistrustful of others, they will pick up on this and they will not be favorably disposed towards you. Instead, find out who you can trust and show these loyal friends and colleagues your appreciation and devotion.

# Chapter Ten - The Peacemaker (Type 9)

## Fifteen Signs You're a Peacemaker

1. Your dearest wish is to avoid conflict at all costs. This makes some people perceive you as agreeable and others view you as too passive.

2. You are an expert at seeing all points of view and every side of the argument.

3. You have difficulty establishing firm personal boundaries.

4. You are capable of bringing warring parties together and can be instrumental in healing conflicts.

5. You may have a tendency to suffer from lower back pain.

6. You have an active interest in the spiritual side of life.

7. When in an intimate relationship, you have a propensity to give up your agenda in favor of your partner's. You tend to merge with your nearest and dearest. This might result in you neglecting your own personal needs and desires.

8. You dislike having to confront the unpleasant aspects of life. Sometimes you run away from them or live in denial.

9. You are likely an introverted person.

10. Your friends would describe you as easy going, reliable, tolerant and likable.

11. Your inclination is to see the best in other people and to have a trusting and optimistic view of life.

12. You probably find great joy and solace in the natural world.

13. You can sometimes be uncomfortable with change and this can cause you to be conservative – but you are more adaptable than you give yourself credit for!

14. Because you are so modest, some people might make the mistake of taking you for granted or overlooking the often significant contributions that you make.

15. You may have been brought up in an environment where you were taught that conflict is bad and something that should be avoided or denied.

Did anything sound familiar? More than one thing? Then you just might be a Peacemaker.

## The Peacemaker Overview

As the name implies, Type Nine on The Enneagram, the Peacemaker, is a seeker of harmony in all areas of life.

Conflict is the enemy itself, as far as the Nine is concerned, and they will avoid it like the plague, if at all feasible. This can be a challenge because, as we all know, conflict is an integral part of life and practically impossible to avoid. So the Peacemaker has to develop strategies to side step these clashes. These often include some manner of withdrawal. This means that Nine is commonly an introvert. Even if the Peacemaker is particularly social, they will find ways to remove themselves from potential strife that may arise within their circle of friends. Because of this, their habit is to go with the flow. Others view them as tolerant and easy going and consequently, easy to like.

The Peacemaker holds a positive view of life and of those that surround them. They are inclined to give people the benefit of the doubt, assuming that they are good sorts until the opposite is proven. They are trusting - as well as trustworthy - and they see the glass as being half-full rather than half-empty. It is common for them to have a stalwart faith - spiritual or otherwise - that things are always working out for them.

A deep-seated desire for the Nine is a sense of connection. They feel this connection with both their fellow humans and with the natural world. The Peacemaker has a genuine connection to nature and will have a sense of being at home wherever it is green. Another arena where the Nine feels at home is parenthood. This type is often an excellent parent - loving and attentive.

Change can sometimes be a challenge for the Type Nine, causing them to feel uneasy and uncomfortable. They do like to stay in their comfort zones! This can translate into quite a conservative attitude towards life. When a Nine is not so well-developed emotionally, they can suffer from a sort of inertia. This can prevent them from taking the action necessary to bring required change into effect. But when change does manifest itself, the Peacemaker may well surprise him or herself with how adaptable they are and how they are, in fact, more than capable of adjusting to their new circumstances. They might also find that they are more resilient than they themselves suspected.

Sometimes they do not give themselves enough credit and this can be quite a problem in their lives. Due to this innate humility and refusal to hog the limelight, the Nine might find him or herself being taken for granted by others. It can almost feel to the Peacemaker like people don't even see them. This lack of validation can be hard to take and they may feel invisible. It is a real shame, as the Peacemaker is capable of and frequently does make significant contributions to many situations. This might show itself as a deep sadness that few are aware of. Or it might be an anger that builds up inside and erupts every so often in a short-lived burst of temper. Or, alternatively, it may reveal itself in passive-aggressive behavior.

It is characteristic of the Nine that they do not always have a definite sense of self and of their own identity. They don't really know who they are! This is only heightened by their penchant to almost merge with their loved ones. They virtually take on the characteristics of those closest to them through a process of identification. So if you are a Nine and you are reading this, it is possible that you do not recognize yourself!

There have been many famous Nines dotted throughout history and prominent in our society today. These include: Queen Elizabeth II, Abraham Lincoln, Carl Jung, Walt Disney, Gloria Steinem, Audrey Hepburn, George Lucas, Princess Grace of Monaco, Claude Monet, Dwight D. Eisenhower, Ronald Reagan, Joseph Campbell, Gary Cooper, Carlos Santana, Tony Bennett, Sophia Loren, Whoopie Goldberg, Geena Davis, Lisa Kudrow, Woody Harrelson, Kevin Costner, Audrey Hepburn, Annette Bening, Jimmy Stewart, Janet Jackson, Ringo Starr, General Colin Powell, John F. Kennedy Jr., Gerald Forde, Norman Rockwell, Jim Henson and John Goodman.

# The Peacemaker Levels

## Healthy

### Self-Possessed

At their peak, Nines are a joy to be around. And it is a joy, in fact, to be one of them! They feel enormously fulfilled by all that life has given them and they are, therefore, supremely content. They feel totally present within themselves. This causes them to have a sense of, not only independence, but an intense aliveness. They are adept at forming profound relationships with others because of this powerful sense of connection.

### Serene

This serenity is often derived from a profound feeling of acceptance. This in turn leads to an enormous sense of stability. They do not doubt themselves and neither do they doubt others. Total trust is the order of the day. There is a perception of ease that they bring to everything that they do, largely because they are patient, good-humored and unselfconscious. They are not trying to be anything that they are not and are genuinely lovely people. There is a simple innocence and a lack of pretense which makes the deeply receptive and healthy Nine a pleasure to be around.

### Supportive

The support that the Peacemaker lends to others carries with it a healing and calming influence. They are fantastic at bringing people together and harmonizing disparate groups. Their optimism reassures others. All the above, together with their often excellent communication skills, can make the Nine a marvellous mediator.

**Neutral**

**Self-Effacing**

This mode of conduct is often designed to avoid conflict as much as possible. They do not want to rock the boat so, consequently, will put up with a lot. They might become accommodating to a fault and go along with other people's wishes. This could make them agree to do things that they really do not want to do. This is not a good scenario for anyone involved!

Another way the Five might seek to avoid rocking the boat is by fitting themselves into conventional roles. They do not relish defying other people's expectations. An example of this is a woman becoming a wife and mother. Then, if she returns to work when her children are older, she might go into a traditionally 'feminine' profession such as nursing or hairdressing. This is not the type that commonly challenges stereotypes.

**Disengaged**

This tendency is due to their wish to avoid problems and conflict of any sort. They might still be taking part in their normal activities but they will be 'checked out' in some way. You might see it in their eyes! They are purposely not paying proper attention. They will not reflect on what is happening because they simply do not want to! They can become complacent, putting up with situations that are not necessarily ideal but are too much trouble to confront. Because of this, they will deny problems and have an impulse to 'sweep them under the rug.' They construct a comforting fantasy world for themselves which is so much more pleasant than reality. The Peacemaker can develop indifference as a coping mechanism, as they refuse to focus on problems and retreat from the real world into self-imposed oblivion.

**Resigned**

This resignation is in a bid to have peace at any price. A kind of fatalism creeps into the atmosphere. Why bother trying to change anything when it will not work anyway? They can be very stubborn in this stance, causing those around them to get annoyed and frustrated with them as they struggle to get a meaningful response or make things happen. They may indulge in wishful thinking and imagine all sorts of possible magical solutions. They will appease others in order to avoid trouble, even when this is not the healthiest solution.

**Unhealthy**

**Repression**

The propensity to hold everything in becomes increasingly unhealthy. It makes the Nine incapable of facing problems as they disassociate themselves from all conflicts. The self cannot be fully actualized in these circumstances and the Peacemaker remains in an undeveloped state. This can actually constitute a danger to those around them as their conduct here can be neglectful.

**Disassociation**

At this point, the Peacemaker disassociates from life to such an extent that they can barely function. A sort of numbness sets in, while they block out awareness of anything that might upset them.

## Catatonic

At this most extreme of lows, the Nine will come across as really disoriented, seemingly becoming nothing more than a shell of their former selves. Psychological conditions can arise, such as schizoid and dependent personality disorders. Multiple personalities are also possible.

## The Peacemaker Wings

### Type Nine with a One wing (9W1)

The Type Nine with a One wing is a big softy! The influence of the Nine will remain mostly dominant, which will result in the intellectuality of the One filtering in, but not being subject to a great deal of reality-testing. This can cause the Nine with a One wing to develop a set of beliefs that might come across as a bit weird to others. They may be strongly superstitious and 'airy fairy.' The Peacemaker with a One wing can actually make this work for them!

The 9W1 is refined and possesses a manner of elegant poise. In style of dress, they will strive to be as inconspicuous as possible, choosing clothing that will enable them to fit in and become as invisible as possible. Mainstream fashion is the order of the day, with no flamboyant statements being made! They do have a desire to be perfect, however, because of their One wing, so their attire is likely to be neat and tidy.

They are not the workaholics of the Enneagram and can be partial to a pleasant afternoon nap!

When in a healthy state of mind, the One wing lends the type Nine more presence. The light is on *and* someone is home! Concrete results are more likely when the goal-setting One wing exerts its influence. The Peacemaker will become more ambitious but will not be prey to as much perfectionism as the Type One in their pure state. By their efforts, this variant of the Type Nine can affect others in a positive and useful way. However, this is done in a subtle, non-showy manner and the world at large might not be aware of what the Nine has done.

At an advanced psychological level, the Nine with a One wing finds great happiness and fulfilment in the work they do, empowering and teaching other people. They no longer feel the urge to withdraw and involve themselves in a meaningful way in the world. Their dreams become reality at last and others feel the full benefit of their self-actualized power.

In a not-so-healthy state, the Nine with the One wing will tend to withdraw in a typical Nine way and become more judgmental of the self and others in a typical One way. They might retreat into a comfortable fantasy world and are inevitably disappointed when their real life interactions do not live up to their fantasies.

When bad goes to worse, they become more upset with the discrepancies between their inner fantasy world and outside reality. They cope with this scenario by isolating themselves. Worst case scenario, they might even become psychotic, where they're barely present in a body that gradually goes to rack and ruin.

It would be quite typical for a Peacemaker with a One wing to find work that allows them to use their mind but not necessarily in a very exacting way. Examples might be astrologers, puppeteers and dressmakers.

**The Type Nine with an Eight wing (9W8)**

These people are the salt of the earth. The Peacemaker with an Eight wing may come across as a little rough-around-the-edges, but cuddly all the same, rather like an over-sized, clumsy puppy, eager for happiness. The inclination is towards gentleness and a lack of sophistication. The Eight will lend the Nine a tad more impulsiveness and forcefulness than they would normally have, but they will back down in the face of too much resistance. The Nine with the Eight wing is not overly eager to rise to every challenge either.

When a Nine with an Eight wing begins to self-actualize, he or she will use their energy and expansiveness to pull themselves out of passivity. They will then become generous, powerful and benevolent.

When fully actualized, the Peacemaker is a truly uplifting presence in the world. They are generous, humble and genuinely good. Just being in their sphere of influence is inspiring. They don't do anything, as such. They are just their wonderful selves.

But it's not all rainbows and unicorns! In a state of stress, the Nine with an Eight wing may be paranoid and become almost hermit like in his or her existence. They will be lazy and mistrustful.

At their absolute lowest level, avoidance becomes paramount as the 9W8 spurns all and any human interaction. It is a kind of semi-comatose state and the paranoid persuasions become worse.

In terms of physical appearance, the Nine with an Eight wing is often big and frequently strong. They will seldom be seen in flashy clothing and will strive for normality.

## Advice for The Peacemaker

1. Body awareness is very important for the Nine. Exercise will help hugely here. It will allow you to discharge aggression and teach you to concentrate and focus your attention. You will become more aware of your feelings and benefit in terms of self-discipline.

2. Repressed anger causes damage, both to your physical and emotional health. Everybody has negative emotions, including you. When you fail to acknowledge this, you can disturb the harmony you so crave in your relationships. It is far healthier for you to be honest about your feelings - both with yourself and with loved ones - and get issues out in the open, fully aired!

3. You find it deeply difficult to examine pain. But looking honestly at why a relationship has gone wrong, and even worse, admitting to possibly contributing to this problem, is necessary, both for your peace of mind and for ensuring that such a situation does not repeat itself. This is how genuine relationships are created.

4. If it is possible to be *too* nice, then you as a Type Nine are arguably the most likely type on the Enneagram to fall into this trap. Not only is it bad for your own sake to be constantly acquiescing to other people's needs, especially with loved ones, it is also bad for the other person and for the relationship as a whole. Keeping the peace can sometimes come at a high price. You have to be yourself to have a successful and genuine relationship. Only when you are completely honest about your own needs can you be truly there for the other person.

5. Daydreaming is not a bad past time per se. However, when overused as a means of tuning out of the world around you, this is not so healthy. You should try to engage with people and participate meaningfully in society.

# Conclusion

So, we come to the end of this book. Have you read it all? Or have you just skipped to your type or the type you *think* you are? Either way is absolutely fine. This book can be taken as a whole or dipped in and out of, as the reader so desires. The approach you take might depend on your type! A meticulous One may peruse each sentence thoroughly from start to finish, whereas an impulsive Seven, might just skip to the "good bits"! It really doesn't matter, as this book is written for each and every type on the Enneagram.

The aim of this book is to give you a thorough understanding of the Enneagram - the theory behind it, its origins, how it works and how it can work for you. You might be guided by what your friends and loved ones have commented about you and your personality over the years or better still, you may be guided by your own self-knowledge. Best of all, you might be led by your own internal guidance system. Whatever the case, this book has the capacity to add to your self-knowledge and your self-awareness. It is up to you to take it on board and to apply it to your own life. Remember, knowledge is power! Not over others but over the self. Self-mastery is key and knowing yourself is of the utmost importance. Applying this knowledge is gold!

We have covered a lot in the preceding chapters. In the introduction, we learned the origins of the word 'enneagram' and the names of the pioneers in the field, devising the methodology and developing the theory into the Enneagram we know today. Of course, many others who were not named throughout these pages have also made important contributions.

The Enneagram is a complex and useful blend of the wisdom of our predecessors and the insights of modern psychology. As such, it can lend a deep understanding of the self, augmenting what we have already learned throughout our life experiences. It can be used for personal growth, for adding spiritual depth, for working out with whom we are compatible and for understanding our close friends and family members in more depth. We can use it in the area of our careers also. So that is why our boss behaves the way he does! Or why that co-worker can sometimes appear so odd! With insight and understanding comes compassion and hopefully, less conflict too.

This book will help you to understand the positives and negatives of each type, both your own and that of all the people around you. Better understanding all round.

Chapter One taught us about the symbol which represents the Enneagram, how it is constructed out of three separate shapes brought together to make one whole. We have the circle, representing the wholeness of life, the triangle, representing the 'magic' number three and the hexad, an unusual, irregular shape, borrowed from the Sufi tradition, representing the law of seven and the law of octaves.

Within the shape are placed the numbers One to Nine which we now know as the nine Types of the Enneagram and the lines on the symbol demonstrate the connections between the different types.

We have further learned that the Enneagram is not a blunt instrument but an exact tool to be wielded subtly. Accordingly, each person is not made of entirely one personality type. The Enneagram gives you wings! You discover your wing by looking at the numbers on either side of yours and ascertaining for yourself which one most closely aligns with you and your unique character.

We then discovered that the Enneagram and its symbol is structured into three separate triads and that each triad holds a different emotion: One, Eight and Nine are rulers of instinct, Two, Three and Four are in the feeling center, and Five, Six and Seven are in the thinking triad.

Enneagram

You will have noticed how each and every chapter begins with a handy check list, allowing you, the reader, to work out as quickly as possible exactly who you are or to point you in the right direction at least. Think of these check lists as sign posts, pointing you towards your correct destination.

You will have learned that when it comes to the Enneagram, it is more likely to be nature rather than nurture which hold the key. A Type appears to be born rather than made and despite the many and varied changes that happen in our lives, our basic type will remain unchanged, as a constant that can be relied upon. And fundamentally, no type is the 'best' type. We can all strive to be the most wonderful version of ourselves.

Along our journey of discovery about The Enneagram, we also found out about the levels. In other words, that there are three basic levels of development in this system: healthy, average or neutral and unhealthy. Therefore, a healthy One, for example, can look like a totally different creature, and indeed type, than an unhealthy One. Each level is, in turn, divided into the sub-levels, in descending or ascending orders, depending on what way you look at it! Yet another example of the subtlety of the Enneagram. Knowing simply which type you are is not knowing the entire story.

It might be helpful to give you a brief summary of the nine different types and the basic characteristics of each one. So, in numerical order and not in order of importance, I give you the Enneagram:

1. Type One is known as the Reformer or the Perfectionist and, as always, these names reveal a great deal. The Reformer values principles and integrity above all and his or her primary motivation is to be both right and good. They strive for perfection at all times and try to maintain self-control. Quality is of utmost importance and the One will appreciate structure and standards.

# Enneagram

The Reformer or Perfectionist has many sterling qualities to offer, such as dignity, discernment, tolerance, serenity and acceptance. Their shadow sides, however, mean that they can be acutely critical of themselves and others, pedantic, uncompromising and judgemental.

2. Type Two is the Helper. Their modus operandi is to be appreciated and liked. They value their relationships above all else and will be generous, kind and self-sacrificing towards this end. They would dearly love to make the world a better place and genuinely try to do this, giving loving attention and support to those they care about. They shine when it comes to being unconditionally supportive. They are also humble beings, who are capable of practicing healthy self-care. On the not-so-plus side, they might be manipulative and flattering in their mode of giving as they strive to get back what they have given.

3. The Achiever, which is Type Three, wants to be the best! Their priorities include results, efficiency, image and recognition. They are capable of being flexible in order to achieve their goals. Anything for success! At his or her best, The Achiever offers those around them hope and integrity. They are also principled, hard working and receptive. At the worst, they can come across as inconstant and self-important. This is because their sense of self is erroneously based on what they do instead of who they are.

4. Type Four, the Individualist, is driven by his or her intense need to express authenticity and uniqueness. Individualism, as the name suggests, is highly valued, as are self-expression, feelings and purpose. They are romantic souls and beauty will be very important to them, as is meaning. The best of the Four is authenticity and equanimity, sensitivity and contentment. The shadow side of the Individualist shows someone who is melancholic, temperamental and believes themselves to be misunderstood.

5. Type Five, the Investigator, is deeply motivated to know and to understand. They love to make sense of the world around them, valuing knowledge and objectivity. Privacy and independence are priorities for this type and at their best, they are mindful and even visionary. But the darker Five is arrogant, stingy and disconnected from their emotions.

6. Type Six, the Loyalists, are very big on belonging and security and their constant drive is to be safe and well-prepared. As the name implies, they value loyalty and trust and they are responsible sorts. The healthy Six is brave and devoted and possesses a sense of inner knowing. When unhealthy, they can be doubting, suspicious or anxious and they may fear letting down their defenses and worry to an excessive level.

7. Type Seven, or the Enthusiast wants to experience all and everything that life has to offer, while avoiding pain in the process. They value freedom and they are optimistic and inspired. Life is a big adventure for the Enthusiast with many opportunities along the way to play and be spontaneous. At their best they are serene and content. At their worst, they can be easily distracted, unfocused, impulsive and uncommitted.

8. Type Eight, the Challenger, only likes to act from a place of strength and dislikes displaying their weaknesses. Control is very important to them and they desire to have an impact in their own direct way. They do love a challenge and will protect those that they perceive to be more vulnerable than themselves. At a healthy level, they are caring, strong and approachable. When unhealthy, they can be aggressive and domineering.

9. Type Nine, or the Peacemaker, wants nothing more than to be in harmony with the world. They place great importance on being

accommodating and accepting. They love peace and stability while hating conflict. At their best, they are vibrant and self-aware. At their worst, they can be stubborn and inclined to procrastinate.

So I hope that you have found the information provided in this book and the way in which it has been presented to be of use to you. The basics have been covered and expanded upon, and a comprehensive and hopefully engaging guide has been provided. I hope that you have managed to identify your personality type and gain self-knowledge in the process. You should now have all the tools at your disposal.

I wish you the very best of luck on your Enneagram journey and indeed, on your journey throughout life. If there is one thing I would love for you to take away from this book, it is this: that there is no such thing as a good type or a bad type. Each personality type encompasses all aspects and no one type is better than another. As we examine our type and the different levels, my hope for all of us is that we strive for the pinnacle of health and maturity, knowing we are meant for better.

www.ingramcontent.com/pod-product-compliance
Lightning Source LLC
Chambersburg PA
CBHW031125080526
44587CB00011B/1117